CHRISTIAN THOUGHT

CHRISTIAN THOUGHT

ITS HISTORY AND APPLICATION

LECTURES WRITTEN FOR DELIVERY
IN ENGLAND DURING MARCH 1923

BY THE LATE
ERNST TROELTSCH
PROFESSOR OF PHILOSOPHY IN THE UNIVERSITY OF BERLIN, AND SOMETIME
PROFESSOR OF THEOLOGY IN THE UNIVERSITY OF HEIDELBERG

TRANSLATED INTO ENGLISH BY VARIOUS HANDS
AND EDITED WITH AN INTRODUCTION AND INDEX BY
BARON F. von HÜGEL
HON. LL.D. (ST. ANDREWS); HON. D.D. (OXFORD)

HYPERION PRESS, INC.
Westport, Connecticut

Published in 1923 by University of London Press, London
Hyperion reprint edition 1979, 1990, 1994
Library of Congress Catalog Number 78-59047
ISBN 0-88355-719-3
Printed in the United States of America

Library of Congress Cataloging in Publication Data
Troeltsch, Ernst, 1865-1923.
  Christian thought, its history and application.

  Translation of Der Historismus und seine
Überwindung.
  Reprint of the 1923 ed. published by University
of London Press.
  Includes index.
  1. Christianity—Addresses, essays, lectures.
I. Hügel, Friedrich, Freiherr von, 1852-1925.
II. Title.
BR83.T7313 1979   170   78-59047
ISBN 0-88355-719-3

PREFATORY NOTE

THE fronts and backs of the several title-pages in this book give all the necessary information concerning Dr. Troeltsch's compositions and our translations of them, respectively. But I want, here, cordially to thank all my kind and zealous collaborators. There are the first translators—Miss Mary E. Clarke (M.A., London), Dr. Maximilian A. Mügge (Göttingen) and his fellow-worker Miss Durban, and Mr. Henry G. Atkins, Professor of German in King's College, London. The first translation of the first *Ethics* lecture is due to myself and to Principal Barker in collaboration. All these first translators were faced by a difficult task, and they all, in various measures and ways, laid the foundations or at least furnished considerable materials towards the final, present text. I must also warmly thank the revisers, who worked so hard to bring the translations into the closest possible touch with the originals and yet to make the English entirely pure and easy.

Professor Clement C. J. Webb and Mr. Edwyn Bevan were here of great help; yet it was Principal Ernest Barker, of King's College, London, who took the lion's share at this stage, making himself responsible for the English of all the three *Ethics* Lectures.

I have also here to thank the men who so generously took the dead author's place, and delivered the several translations of his lectures in the places where, alive, he would have delivered them himself. Professor Clement C. J. Webb was able, at Oxford, to keep also to the day originally fixed for the *Christianity* lecture. Principal Ernest Barker and Mr. Edwyn Bevan, respectively, read the three *Ethics* lectures and the *Politics* lecture, on various dates in May, the former at King's College, London, the latter before a meeting of the *London Society for the Study of Religion*.

I myself have everywhere kept the closest watch over the special meanings, often far from easy, of Dr. Troeltsch's texts. I sincerely trust that the Lectures now appear here with an unbroken, very close fidelity to the originals, and yet read very nearly as if they were not translations but originals.

The Introduction has cost me much labour, especially also as an act both of fearless fidelity to my own best lights and of devoted, interpretative love for the man who ought here to eclipse us all. I have been much helped by the criticisms of my kind, close friend Professor Norman Kemp Smith of Edinburgh University and of Principal Ernest Barker, whom I trust to have gained as a friend over this our common task, in which he has helped so predominantly much.

The Index is by myself: I have tried to make it sufficiently rich in cross references to be of real use.

We owe warm thanks to Mr. W. Stanley Murrell, the Manager of the University of London Press, for much patience and generosity towards our several demands: his helpfulness throughout has greatly aided such success as we may have attained.

F. v. H.

Dr. Troeltsch left no indication concerning a common title for these lectures, all carefully entitled by himself.

Professor Clement C. J. Webb proposed: *History and Religion* or *Religion and History*.

Principal Ernest Barker suggested: *History and Application of Christian Thought.* I myself merely inverted Dr. Barker's title, which so well expresses the treble characteristic of Dr. Troeltsch's mind.

F. v. H.

CONTENTS

SECTION I

THE PLACE OF CHRISTIANITY AMONG THE WORLD-RELIGIONS: A LECTURE WRITTEN FOR DELIVERY BEFORE THE UNIVERSITY OF OXFORD 1

SECTION II

ETHICS AND THE PHILOSOPHY OF HISTORY: THREE LECTURES WRITTEN FOR DELIVERY BEFORE THE UNIVERSITY OF LONDON

1. THE MORALITY OF THE PERSONALITY AND OF THE CONSCIENCE . . 37
2. THE ETHICS OF THE CULTURAL VALUES 69
3. THE COMMON SPIRIT . . . 101

SECTION III

POLITICS, PATRIOTISM, AND RELIGION: A LECTURE WRITTEN FOR DELIVERY BEFORE THE LONDON SOCIETY FOR THE STUDY OF RELIGION 131

INDEX 169

INTRODUCTION

THE main history of this little book is easily told. Professor Ernst Troeltsch had, ever since at least 1901, when I first came to know him, longed to visit the England whose philosophy, politics, and religion he knew, in their literature and history, so astonishingly well. But one obstacle after another arose, and forced him repeatedly to adjourn the visit, till the Great War came and rendered impossible all such schemes for another eight years or more. At last, all seemed settled for a ten days' visit during March of this year, and the five lectures here printed were written last December and January, to be then translated into English and delivered by himself in Oxford, London, Edinburgh, and again in London. The further details concerning these lectures, originals and translations, will be found on the two sides of the title-pages immediately preceding the three constituents of the book.

Ernst Troeltsch's antecedents, environment,

and career may be stated in a few words. He
sprang from an ancient burgher family, settled
for centuries in the Lausitz between Swabia
and Bavaria, and more recently at Nürnberg
and Augsburg in Bavaria itself. His father
was a physician practising in Augsburg, and
there the eldest son, Ernst, was born in 1865.
From 1883 to 1888 he studied Protestant
Theology at Erlangen, Göttingen, and Berlin,
and was most influenced by Albrecht Ritschl.
He next served for some time as an Evange-
lical (Lutheran) curate in Munich; became
Lecturer at Göttingen in 1891, Extraordinary
Professor in Bonn University in 1892; and
already in 1894 obtained the Ordinary (full)
Professorship of Systematic Theology at Heidelberg, where he remained 21 years. There
he wrote almost all his abidingly important
minor works, and especially his only complete,
large, now standard, book, *The Social Doctrines
of the Christian Churches and Groups* (1912);
and whilst there he sat for many years as an
elected member in the Baden Upper House.
It was there that, after studying his writings
for five years, I first communicated with
him and visited him in April 1901. He
married, a month later, the daughter of a
Mecklenburg landed proprietor and officer.
They had to wait over twelve years for the

birth of their only child, Ernst Eberhard, in July 1913.

At Easter 1915 he succeeded in Berlin to the Philosophical Chair of Otto Pfleiderer and Edvin Lehmann; and there he lectured on the Philosophy of Religion, Ethics, Philosophy of General Civilisation, Introduction to Philosophy, History of Modern Philosophy, and Philosophy of History. From 1919 to 1921 he was a member of the Prussian Landtag and Under-Secretary of State in the Ministry of Public Worship.

He just lived to see published the concluding part of the first volume of his second large work, *The Historical Standpoint and its Problems (der Historismus und seine Probleme)*, in January of this year. The three lectures for the University of London are anticipations of what was to have been the central theme of the second volume of this work, a volume all unwritten excepting the sketch here presented.

As to Dr. Troeltsch's religious and philosophical outlook, I shall confine myself to those points which appear prominently in the following lectures or which may be strictly necessary for understanding their origin and character; but I want first to suggest three general considerations. The first is that we shall do no credit to the memory of this assuredly great man unless we study him in something of the spirit with which he studied others and appraised himself. In his many letters to me he returned again and again to his own very certain limitations, to his fear lest I should overestimate him, and, above all, to his being but a fallible seeker after truth, who thinking and writing so much upon the most difficult of problems ran very real risks of committing grave mistakes. Dr. Albert Dietrich, his chief Berlin disciple, in a strikingly lifelike sketch, describes how Troeltsch, a student among his own students, would, when he was conscious of having gone astray, himself promptly point out his error; indeed, would, amidst mutual surprise and laughter, openly change the direction or procedure of an entire course, however long and laborious this course had already been. "Always ready to learn and to relearn, he recoiled from nothing more than from airs of having spoken the last word. . . . And though doubts have repeatedly been expressed as to the value of this extremely personal relation to University students, the training power inherent in the subjects of study, when thus treated under his leadership, never failed to vindicate itself victoriously."[1] Such a man is unfairly dealt with if we hesitate to test his conclusions with all possible rigour—it may be suspending our judgment, or even, after much careful consideration, giving it against him with the genial candour that has so often impelled him to remain uncertain or even to conclude against himself.

The second preliminary will be sufficiently illustrated in what follows: Dr. Troeltsch changed considerably after the time when I knew his mind so intimately — after the *Soziallehren* (1912) and especially after the outbreak of the War (August 1914). The change has been mostly away from what, till then, we had in common—from the reality, helpfulness, indeed necessity of at least some tradition ; from recognition that various spiritual facts exist and are apprehensible by us, before our act and habit of faith ; and from the perception that the fruits which follow and justify our act and habit of faith are, in part, visible to others, not to ourselves alone. I do not doubt that he deeply felt the isolation of his country from the rest of the world, and perhaps even more painfully, the loneliness of himself amidst many of his own people, and

[1] *Ernst Troeltsch*, by Dr. A. D., *Archiv f. Politik u. Geschichte*, Berlin, March 1923.

would thereby be influenced in the direction of this excessive individualism—excessive, surely, in so realistic a believer in God and in the need and power of His help as Troeltsch remained up to the very end of his life. As late as July 1922 he wrote: " Man, thank God, possesses a second Fatherland from which no one can cast him out. In this other country we are both of us at home." Elsewhere he tells me of the fearful strain which the writing of the last part of the *Historismus* had cost him.

The changes traceable in the later Troeltsch are, however, all covered by the phrase appearing in these lectures " I have, in such matters, become more and more radical." For, indeed, already in 1901 he clearly implied to me his holding the view just indicated concerning the act of faith—that none of its evidences preceded it, but that it all followed from the act; and again, he then expressly declared to me his inability to recognise Church and Sacraments as legitimate continuations or developments of our Lord's mind, although he fully realised St. Paul's emphatic teaching and practice of these things. Yet up to 1914, in the spirit of his *Fundamental Problems of Ethics* (1902), he could be absorbed in directly constructive thinking and remain practically untouched by these emphatic individualisms.

But although his faith in God remained grandly vigorous and touchingly direct from first to last, yet none the less his attempts at a philosophical formulation of this faith showed, at the end, traces of the pressure exercised upon his mind by the Individualism which, up to then, had not sufficiently preponderated to incline him to such formulation. This faith in God and the ceaseless sense of the Spirit of Jesus evidently sprang from the very earliest impressions which a Christian home and an unusually gifted and forceful mother could not fail to produce in so reverent and hungry a soul as was his own.

The third preliminary concerns our own English mentality. Dr. Troeltsch here also assuredly meant to be quite fair; indeed, in the lecture entitled "Politics" he is even generous. Nevertheless his very strange omission of all mention of the English Hegelians, and of other Idealist thinkers such as Dr. F. H. Bradley and Professor James Ward, leaves English thought represented here, during the last two generations, by Mill and Spencer alone. Indeed, English thought here continuously forms, with French thought, the "West-European Mind" in contrast with the "German Mind," in so far as that is idealist. Yet the influence of T. H. Green (d. 1882) has, in Britain, been very great, so too that of R. Lewis Nettleship (d. 1892); and, precisely in connection with Dr. Troeltsch's main theme, B. Bosanquet (d. 1923) has given us the Gifford Lectures on "The Principle of Individuality and Value" and on "The Value and Destiny of the Individual" (1912, 1913). The English Hegelians are at least as different from Hegel and his German followers as were the Roman Stoics from their Greek predecessors; Green, especially, was a personality hard to equal anywhere—indeed, the school at large is a striking exhibition of markedly English characters full of a philosophy as lofty and unworldly as any produced by Germany.

The lecture on the " Place of Christianity among the World Religions " is the most ambitious as it is also doubtless the most contentious of all the constituents of this volume. Dr. Troeltsch has here restated the positions of his *Absolute Validity of Christianity* (1909), and these positions still appear to me very true and strong; but the new attitude of the lecture itself, while raising further questions in a delicate and astonishingly living manner—his tender attitude towards the higher non-Christian World Religions resembles that of the great German Renaissance Cardinal Nicolas Cusanus, with his proposed alliance between Christianity and Islam against materialism and indifference—yet leaves my mind unsatisfied upon the following fundamental questions.

It was in the *Separation of State and Church* (1907), so sober and satisfying in its main contention, that Troeltsch first introduced the very difficult, indeed I believe ultimately impossible, conception of "*polymorphous* truth." He there contends that the Old Church alone retains, with full consciousness and final self-commitment, the conception of Truth as essentially *monomorphous*. Against this he holds that while God, indeed, is one, and all Truth, as it is in Him, is but one, that Truth as apprehended, or even as apprehensible, by man varies indefinitely from race to race and from age to age, and does so in *quality* no less than in quantity. We can trace no element in any part of our knowledge, not even in our mathematics, which remains identical through all our earthly space and time.

It is this doctrine, I am convinced, which now, more than anything else, gives to Troeltsch's general outlook a curiously double aspect, and this in despite of the obvious simplicity of the man, and indeed of the strong

realism persistently characteristic of his deepest
convictions and of his touchingly ardent seek-
ings. For this " polymorphous " truth, without doubt, belongs intrinsically to the nomina-
list outlook, a fact indicated by the straining
insistence, now curiously apparent in Dr.
Troeltsch, that this chameleon-like truth—this
truth utterly different for different times and
races—is, nevertheless, Truth and Life in very
deed, and forms a reliable vehicle for God to
man and for man to God. But how can this
be ? I behold an orange and I do so by seeing,
simultaneously both its particulars and what it
shares with the lemon and the lime. The
family of citrate fruits is as little a mere
creation of my mind as are the orange, the
lemon, and the lime in their distinctions each
from the others and from the family of which,
notwithstanding, they are members. The
general citrate qualities, affinities, effects do
not indeed exist separately, but all the same
they do exist within the particulars as really
as these orange, lemon, lime particulars exist
within the general citrate qualities. So with
my dog, and foxes, jackals, wolves ; so with
my cat, the lion, the leopard, and the tiger.
Dr. Troeltsch would, doubtless, demur to such
a comparison between facts of the physical and
animal world and the deep spiritual realities,

those various apprehensions by the finite human spirits of the infinite Spirit, God. Yet a similar mixture of general and particular, where the general is no less real than the particular, though not separable from it, is surely observable in the religions of the world. Dr. Troeltsch maintains that the Russian Church is *utterly* different from the Latin Church, and *a fortiori*, of course, that Christianity, taken as a whole, is *utterly* different from Judaism and Mohammedanism. Yet how can we fail to find real qualities really common to all the ancient episcopal, sacramental Christian bodies—qualities as real as are the qualities peculiar to the Roman Catholic Church, to the Græco-Russian Church, and to the other similar institutional Christian bodies severally?

Just as in thus looking back to what was, or around to what is, we find in Troeltsch's outlook no general qualities really extant together with the particulars which here alone are real, so in looking forward any one thing may, for him, become in any way any other; e.g. it is, he argues, impossible to foresee what Christianity may become in the course of time. I cannot but greatly prefer his minute study of the kinships and contrasts between Lutheranism and Calvinism in the *Kultur der Gegenwart*

(1906, 1909) and the confident prophecy as to what cannot change or perish in Christianity with which the *Soziallehren* (1912) concludes so majestically. I find that only if I take Dr. Troeltsch's latter-day supreme richness of historical outlook and psychological analysis as the introduction to his earlier metaphysical conclusions, with their philosophical articulation and steady clarity, can I escape from admitting that a certain impression conveyed by Dr. Troeltsch's later writings accurately represents the necessary outcome of them all. Professor Friedrich Meinecke, that finely religious-tempered historian, the close companion of Dr. Troeltsch's latest years, in his mature and balanced *Ernst Troeltsch und das Problem des Historismus* (Berlin: "Deutsche Nation," March 1923), tells us: " His friends, who were devoted to him in admiration and in love, and who have lost in him one of the most affluent sources of light for their life, have nevertheless when they exchanged their impressions of him among themselves, been driven to confess that his positive leading ideas and aims stood in a certain disproportion to the amazing riches of his speculative historical outlook; and that his weighty speech would often curiously ebb away when, at the end of impressive reproductions of the life and thoughts of others, he was put to develop his own position in a firm, clear, and unambiguous manner." Let me ask, in all grateful, regretful simplicity, how, in view of that excessive individualism, which all but completely mastered him in recent years, it could be otherwise. Midas died of hunger from his fatal gift of turning all he touched into gold ; so also Troeltsch, *qua* vehement individualist, finds himself incapable of deriving spiritual force and food from those entrancing historical perspectives which everywhere arise under his magical touch. Since each such scene is utterly unique, we are left without common standard, or common ideal— the entire collection, however intellectually interesting, can afford no aid towards the establishment of an act and habit of faith. A sheer *salto mortale*, clear outside of and above all these fertile scenes, a leap into what is visible indeed after the dread leap, but even then visible to the leaper alone : this is indeed a disconcertingly jejune ending to such historical researches so eagerly pursued. The wonder is only that the conclusion does not appear more thin than it does in fact appear. But then we have to do with a soul of the rarest richness which, in spite of every logical self-entrapment, does partly have its way ; and again this soul retains certain grand convictions, alive still, from pre-individualistic days—its faith in God and its sense of Christ—convictions assuredly *not* acquired by such a break-neck plunge.

Yet, in this lecture, Dr. Troeltsch is also giving expression to a very precious truth, never to be forgotten as against the extension of natural science concepts to the moral and spiritual realities: namely, that these latter, with their special costliness and greater differentiation, have richer values running throughout their several entireties, so that none of them possesses any doctrine or practice simply identical and completely interchangeable with the corresponding doctrine or practice of any other. Nevertheless, these religions and religious institutions cannot consist of differences alone; the differences must appear within some common qualities: for how otherwise could Dr. Troeltsch so acutely feel these religions to be different? Every comparison, of no matter what two things, involves some element common to these two things. It would surely be simpler to insist upon the utter unknowableness of all religions, indeed of all that, according to him, is entirely individual, i.e. of everything that exists at all, than thus to insist that objects of any kind, sufficiently known by us for even the simplest predication, are, or ever can be, utterly unique. And, indeed, Dr. Troeltsch himself repeatedly implies, and occasionally even clearly admits, that the religions of the world *are* comparable, that there *is* an affinity between them—i.e. that they possess certain common qualities.

The three lectures " Ethics and the Philosophy of History " are especially helpful in their steady and penetrating discrimination between the Morality of Conscience and the Ethic of the Cultural Values specially prominent in Lectures 1 and 2. Assuredly there cannot easily be too emphatic an insistence upon the distinction, upon the necessity to develop both, and upon the fact that only when we come to fill that morality with this ethic and to penetrate this ethic with that morality, do we reach the central difficulty, and so penetrate to the full, living fruitfulness of ethical practice or of ethical theory. Already in 1902 he had, in his *Fundamental Problems of Ethics*, magnificently insisted upon the same point in detailed application to our Lord's teaching, and had thus definitely reacted against a prominent doctrine of Ritschlianism old and new. I am well aware that Hegel, in his *Philosophy of Right* (Second Part, Third Section), published in 1833, makes the same point against Kant; yet Dr. Troeltsch gives us, I should maintain, a far more adequate outlook, in that he remains free from the Monism which, whatever were the intentions of Hegel and his followers, so deeply penetrates their philosophical thought.

There is here also the striking doctrine of Group Personalities, a doctrine doubtless derived from the great works of von Gierke, and which has been so brilliantly championed among ourselves by the late Professor F. W. Maitland. Only thus do we leave the eighteenth-century atomism completely behind us, and find a fully adequate reason for the person-building power of the great social groups—the Family, the Guild, the State, the Church.

The third "Ethics" lecture is deeply instructive in its persistent endeavour to attain the power and peace of a common mind, by means which are frankly and sheerly individualist in character. I turn back for what I find lacking here to his own profound explanation in the *Soziallehren* of the deep significance of Infant Baptism; that it stands for the all-important fact of our attainment to personality, in the first instance all but entirely, and up to the end very largely, through our birth and incorporation into a world of realised values, a world already awake to and penetrated by that spiritual life which, as yet, only slumbers within ourselves. I greatly wish that the later over-absorption in the individual contribution (real though it certainly is in conviction of every kind) had not pushed so very much aside this great insight into these other, more extensive and equally necessary means and conditions of all growth. To see in such traditional training and illumination nothing but oppression and *Eleatic* fixity is as little just as it would be to see nothing but revolt and *Heracleitan* evaporation in that element of individual spontaneity, appropriation, and risk by which Dr. Troeltsch had become so greatly impressed. That pre-existing, already awake and awakening world of the Spirit, and this later awakening single spirit, belong together, and the steady aim of our inquiry must surely be to determine how they act and react, completing each other: neither Parmenides nor Heracleitus, but only Plato, inclusive of the truths of both, is adequate to real life.

I believe this one-sidedness to spring in part from a curious oversight, which Dr. Troeltsch shares with Professor Eucken. Both these thinkers write as though the new fruitfulness observed by the new believer as springing from his faith were an object of cognition for the neophyte alone, whereas it is certainly visible, more or less, to others as well ; and that in such manner it can, and does, remain stored in tradition for other places and for other times. What, from the first, gained more men to faith than probably all other reasons put together is surely the evidence, standing clear before them, of the practical, indeed also the speculative, fruitfulness of such faith in the believers known to them. These non-believers have not risked all in utter darkness and then experienced, themselves alone, the fruitfulness of such an act. But they have first seen numerous instances of such fruitfulness in others ; and then, when they have made and whilst they are maintaining this act of faith, they not only see fruitfulness in themselves, but they show it also to others. Only thus can we understand the survival across the centuries of the great religions, and especially of Christianity. There is now in Dr. Troeltsch a straining, an unrest, a vehemence, honourable indeed to the generous man who persisted thus in a faith supposed by him attainable only by such ceaseless, costly tension ; but which, in the actual lives of the great heroes of faith, never forms more than a part, and usually a smaller part, of their means to faith and of the temper of mind thereby attained.

Surely, also, we here again find a certain strange obtuseness with regard to the institutional element of religion. The persistent capacity of institutional religions for nourishing and training strong souls to greater strength appears here to be directly shattered by historical criticism, as though these religions possess no worthy power save in so far as they teach a critically correct history of their own origins. The modern man here seems to be represented as having no genuine need of the Church, and the Church as having nothing left to give him. Yet we have so thoroughly modern-minded a philosopher as the late Professor Royce to warn us how directly attractive can be to some such souls the virtues specially cultivated, and indeed in part cultivable only, within the " Beloved Community " —the Church. Thus, in his last course of lectures, " The Problem of Christianity " (1913), Dr. Royce can tell us (page 15): " James [William James in his *Varieties of Religious Experience*] supposed that the religious experiences of a church must needs be conventional, and consequently must be lacking in depth and in sincerity. This to my mind was a profound and momentous error in the whole religious philosophy of our greatest American master in the study of the psychology of religious experience."

The last constituent of this book, " Politics, Patriotism, and Religion," is, I believe, quite free from anything that need raise serious difficulties in other religious minds ; indeed, the concluding pages seem to me of a directness, courage, and far-seeing discrimination most necessary for us everywhere, yet very rare in every country. The distinction he draws between Patriotism as felt and lived by the unsophisticated mind, and the scheme superinduced upon it by legalists and politicians across the centuries, could hardly have come from a professional politician, nor is it likely rapidly to gain recruits amongst the average readers of the newspapers. Yet it may well, even now, approve itself to some thoughtful minds as part of the wisdom of the higher politics.

Steele, writing in Queen Anne's time, concludes his sketch of a young lady, beautiful and innocent, sensitive and yet full of outward-looking interest and kindness, with the famous exclamation " To love her is a liberal education!" Surely, in all times and places, the most ready, yet also the most costly way of learning deeply, that is, of growing in our very questions, and in our whole temper of mind, is to learn in admiration of some other living fellow-man, recognised by us as more gifted, or more trained, or more experienced than ourselves. Thus did Providence give Dr. Troeltsch also to myself to learn from, as now his Berlin disciples have been growing under that rarely noble inspiration. Not one of us could, I believe, swear to every one of his much-varying opinions. But to confront, even in sheer non-acceptance, this or that position of so great a mind after having repeatedly tried sincerely to adopt it, can perhaps be as fruitful an experience as when he taught us so much in days past. May the students of this little book, in their degree and way, converse, ruminate, remonstrate with him; may they go thus regretfully against him or joyfully with him as one still alive, and still abundantly enlivening, in our present midst.

FRIEDRICH VON HÜGEL.

KENSINGTON.
Midsummer Day, 1923.

SECTION I
DIE STELLUNG DES CHRISTENTUMS UNTER DEN WELTRELIGIONEN

A Lecture written for delivery before the University of Oxford on the invitation of Professor Clement C. J. Webb, *March* 1923.

*THE PLACE OF CHRISTIANITY AMONG
THE WORLD-RELIGIONS*

Translated by MISS MARY E. CLARKE, *Graduate in
Philosophy of the University of London.*

Carefully revised by BARON F. VON HÜGEL *and*
PROFESSOR CLEMENT C. J. WEBB.

I

THE PLACE OF CHRISTIANITY AMONG THE WORLD-RELIGIONS

It has long been my great desire to visit the famous University of Oxford, which shines across to us in my country with the splendour of its mediæval days, and is most closely associated for us with the problem of the development of Nominalism and Empiricism out of the Scholastic philosophy. But that it would be my privilege to survey it from the height of an Oxford lecture-platform was a thing which exceeded my boldest aspirations. I am indebted for this high honour to Professor Clement C. J. Webb, and to the kind interest which you have shown in my literary work. I am deeply conscious how great an honour it is, and I should like to offer you and Mr. Webb my very sincere thanks. I can only hope that you will not miss to-day the wisdom and learning of your ordinary teacher.

In view of these unusual circumstances, I could not select any other subject than the one which contains the centre and starting-point of my academic work. This central theme is most clearly, I think, set forth in my little book on *The Absolute Validity of Christianity*, which forms the conclusion of a series of earlier studies and the beginning of new investigations of a more comprehensive kind in the philosophy of history. Moreover, this subject is for me the point at which my own original interests and the problems presented by the modern religious situation have met together. It was recognised as such by a countryman of your own, Mr. A. C. Bouquet, in his book *Is Christianity the Final Religion?* and I am indebted to him for a very able statement and criticism of the position. I should like, therefore, to occupy this hour in explaining the position I adopted in my little book, and in elucidating the further development of my thought by means of this same small work.

To put it briefly, the central meaning of this book consists in a deep and vivid realisation of the clash between historical reflection and the determination of standards of truth and value. The problem thus arising presented itself to me at a very early age. I had

had a predominantly humanistic and historical education, from which I had been led to extend my studies and interests over a wide field of historical investigation, using the terms "history" and "humanity" in the sense we in Germany have been wont to attribute to them in our best periods—namely, in the objective sense of a contemplation of objects which covers as far as possible the whole extent of human existence, and which finds its delight in all the abundant diversity and ceaseless movement characteristic of human existence, and this without seeking any precise practical ends. It seems to us that it is the wealth of moral life and development that manifests itself in this endlessly diversified world of history, and imparts some of its own loftiness and solemnity to the soul of the observer.

I was, however, inspired by another interest, which was quite as strong and quite as much a part of my natural endowment as the first, I mean the interest in reaching a vital and effective religious position, which could alone furnish my life with a centre of reference for all practical questions, and could alone give meaning and purpose to reflection upon the things of this world. This need of mine led me to theology and philosophy, which I devoured with an equally passionate interest. I soon discovered, however, that the historical studies which had so largely formed me, and the theology and philosophy in which I was now immersed, stood in sharp opposition, indeed even in conflict, with one another. I was confronted, upon the one hand, with the perpetual flux of the historian's data, and the distrustful attitude of the historical critic towards conventional traditions, the real events of the past being, in his view, discoverable only as a reward of ceaseless toil, and then only with approximate accuracy. And, upon the other hand, I perceived the impulse in men towards a definite practical standpoint—the eagerness of the trusting soul to receive the divine revelation and to obey the divine commands. It was largely out of this conflict, which was no hypothetical one, but a fact of my own practical experience, that my entire theoretical standpoint took its rise.

Though this conflict was a personal one, however, it was no mere accident of my personal experience. It was rather the personal form in which a vital problem characteristic of the present stage of human development presented itself to me. I am of course aware that the sting of this problem is not equally felt in all parts of the civilised world of Europe and America. As Bouquet has explained in the work I have already mentioned, we must not apply without reservation to England, still less to America with its very undeveloped historical sense, what is true, in this respect, of other countries.

Nevertheless, there exists at bottom, everywhere, an impression that historical criticism and the breadth of historical interest are fraught with danger to the recognition of simple standards of value, be they of rational or traditional origin. In the Anglo-Saxon countries it is especially ethnography and the comparative study of religion, together with careful philosophical criticism, that produce this attitude. In my own country it is primarily an examination of European civilisation itself that has impressed us with the relativity and transitoriness of all things, even of the loftiest values of civilisation. The effect, however, is very similar in the two cases. Whether we approach it from the standpoint of Herbert Spencer and the theory of evolution, or from that of Hegel and Ranke and German romanticism, history presents a spectacle of bewildering diversity, and of historical institutions as all in a perpetual state of movement from within.

Indeed, the comparative study of religion, which gives an additional impulse to the tendency to relativity produced by historical reflection, has been pre-eminently the work of the great colonising nations, especially of the English and the Dutch. And the criticism of the Bible and of dogma is not without representatives in England ; and thus a growing feeling of uncertainty has been created here in this department also. The difference between this English line of reflection and the historical thought of Germany really consists simply in the fact that the latter is less wont to consider the practical needs and interests of society, whilst in theory it is determined more by the concept of individuality than by sociological or evolutionary principles which tend to regard all processes as leading to a single goal presented by nature.

Important as these differences are, however, they are all but different aspects of the one fundamental conflict between the spirit of critical scepticism generated by the ceaseless flux and manifold contradictions within the sphere of history and the demand of the religious consciousness for certainty, for unity, and for peace. Whether this conflict becomes more apparent in the critical analysis of details or in the challenging of fundamental principles, the cause and the general effect remain very much the same.

In my book on *The Absolute Validity of Christianity* I examined the means whereby theology is able to defend itself against these difficulties. This of course involved an examination of the fundamental concepts of theology as such. I believed that I could here determine two such concepts, both of which claimed to establish the ultimate validity of the Christian revelation in opposition to the relativities revealed by the study of history.

The first of these concepts was the theory that the truth of Christianity is guaranteed by miracles. In our times we are no longer primarily concerned here with miracles in the external world, i.e. with the so-called "nature-miracles," involving an infringement of natural law, but with the miracles of interior conversion and the attainment of a higher quality of life through communion with Jesus and His community. In this connection, it is claimed, an entirely different type of causation comes into operation from that which is operative anywhere else in the world. The Christian life may indeed be compared to an island in the midst of the stream of history, exposed to all the storms of secular life, and lured by all its wiles, yet constituting, in reality, a stronghold of experience of quite another order. The absolute validity of Christianity rests upon the absoluteness of God Himself, who is made manifest here directly in miracles but who manifested Himself beyond this island only as a *causa remota*—as the ground of the inter-connection of all relative things. In this way both a natural and a supernatural theology are possible, the latter resting upon the new birth and experience of the inner man, whilst natural theology is based upon the facts and forces of the external world. This theory is simply a restatement of the old miracle apologetic in the more intimate and spiritual form which it acquired under the influence of Methodism and Pietism.

The second fundamental concept of theology, which I have called the concept of evolution, presents a considerable contrast to the first. Its most important exponent is Hegel. According to this view Christianity is simply the perfected expression of religion as such. In the universal process of the unfolding of Spirit, the fundamental impulse towards salvation and communion with God overcomes all the limitations of sense experience, of the natural order, of mythological form, until it attains perfect expression in Christianity, and enters into combination with the loftiest and most spiritual of all philosophies, namely, that of Platonism. Christianity, it is maintained, is not *a particular* religion, it is *religion*. It is no isolated manifestation of Spirit, but the flower of spiritual life itself. All religion implies salvation and re-birth, but outside Christianity these are subject to the limitations of physical nature and are baulked by human selfishness. In the prophets and in Christ the Divine Life breaks through these limits and flows unrestrained into the thirsty world, which finds therein the solution of all its conflicts and the goal of all its striving. The whole history of religion and its obvious trend are thus a completely adequate proof of Christianity. The historical process does not stand in opposition to it. When regarded as a whole, and as one process, it rather affords a demonstration of its supreme greatness and all-embracing power. The miracles which attend its development are partly explicable, as in other religions, as mythical elements, accumulated during the growth of tradition, but they are partly effects of the shock produced by the spiritual revolution traceable here. They are thus not so much its credentials as its attendant phenomena, and as such they may be left without anxiety in the hands of the historical critic.

I found myself obliged to dismiss both these views as untenable. The former I rejected on the ground that an inward miracle, though it is indeed a powerful psychical upheaval, is not a miracle in the strict sense of the term. Are we justified in tracing the Platonic *Eros* to a natural cause, whilst we attribute a supernatural origin to the Christian *Agape*? And how can we prove such origin, even if we care to assume it? This would only be possible by having recourse once more to the visible signs which accompany these inward miracles, which would be again to treat the accompaniment as if it were itself the melody. Moreover, we should then be faced with the competition furnished by similar miracles in the non-Christian religions, not to mention the negative results of historical criticism and the trouble attendant upon every theory of miracles.

If, however, we turn for this reason to the second view, we find the difficulties to be different, indeed, but no less formidable. The actual history of religion knows nothing of the common character of all religions, or of their natural upward trend towards

Christianity. It perceives a sharp distinction between the great world-religions and the national religions of heathen tribes, and further discovers certain irresolvable contradictions between these world-religions themselves which render their ultimate fusion and reconciliation in Christianity highly improbable, either in theory or in practice. Moreover, Christianity is itself a theoretical abstraction. It presents no historical uniformity, but displays a different character in every age, and is, besides, split up into many different denominations, hence it can in no wise be represented as the finally attained unity and explanation of all that has gone before, such as religious speculation seeks. It is rather a particular, independent, historical principle, containing, similarly to the other principles, very diverse possibilities and tendencies.

This leads us finally to a conception which has, I think, obtained less recognition in other countries than in Germany—I mean the conception which dominates the whole sphere of history, viz. Individuality. History cannot be regarded as a process in which a universal and everywhere similar principle is confined and obscured. Nor is it a continual mixing and remixing of elemental psychical powers, which indicate a general trend of things towards a rational end or goal of evolution. It is rather an immeasurable, incomparable profusion of always-new, unique, and hence individual tendencies, welling up from undiscovered depths, and coming to light in each case in unsuspected places and under different circumstances. Each process works itself out in its own way, bringing ever-new series of unique transformations in its train, until its powers are exhausted, or until it enters as component material into some new combination. Thus the universal law of history consists precisely in this, that the Divine Reason, or the Divine Life, within history, constantly manifests itself in always-new and always-peculiar individualisations—and hence that its tendency is not towards unity or universality at all, but rather towards the fulfilment of the highest potentialities of each separate department of life. It is this law which, beyond all else, makes it quite impossible to characterise Christianity as the reconciliation and goal of all the forces of history, or indeed to regard it as anything else than an historical individuality.

These are the historical ideas which have been handed down to us from German Romanticism, the great opposition movement to Rationalism and to all the clumsy miracle

CHRISTIANITY AMONG WORLD-RELIGIONS 15

apologetic. They illustrate the special character and significance of German Romanticism, considered as a part of the great Romantic Movement of Europe. They form the starting point of all the German history and most of the German theology of the nineteenth century. They present our problem in its most crucial form, and explain why it became a more burning problem in Germany than elsewhere, except where it was envisaged in the same way, either as a result of independent reflection or under German influence.

What, then, is the solution? This is the question which I attempted to answer in my book. I first endeavoured to show that it was in any case impossible to return to the old miracle apologetic. This has been rendered untenable, not by theories, but by documents, by discoveries, by the results of exploration. The force of such evidence cannot be resisted by anyone whose sense of truth has been educated by philology, or even by anyone possessing an average amount of ordinary "common sense." I then submitted that the mere fact of the universality of Christianity —of its presence in all the other religions— would, even if true—be irrelevant. The point at issue was not whether Christianity was as a matter of fact universal, or at least implicit in all religion, but whether it possessed ultimate truth, a truth which might easily depend upon a single instance of itself.

This formed a position for further reflection. It is quite possible, I maintained, that there is an element of truth in every religion, but that this is combined with innumerable transitory, individual features. This element of truth can only be disentangled through strife and disruption, and it should be our constant endeavour to assist in this process of disentanglement. The recognition of this truth is, however, an intuition which is born of deep personal experience and a pure conscientiousness. No strict proof of it is possible, for to demonstrate the actual presence of this truth in all the other cases would not be to establish its validity, even if this demonstration were easier than it is. Such an intuition can only be confirmed retrospectively and indirectly by its practical fruits, and by the light that it sheds upon all the problems of life. Thus in relation to Christianity such an intuition can only arise from immediate impression and personal conviction. Its claim to universal validity can only be felt and believed, in the first instance, and must be confirmed retrospectively through its genuine ability to furnish a solution of the various problems of life.

Now, validity of this kind seems always to rest upon the fine point of personal conviction. We still require a broader foundation upon actual, objective facts. I believed that I had discovered such a foundation for Christianity in the terms in which its claim to ultimate validity finds instinctive and immediate expression; in other words, in its faith in revelation and in the kind of claim it makes to truth. I thought it necessary to compare it from this point of view with other religions, whose belief in revelation and claim to validity were in every case of quite a different kind. If we examine any of the great world-religions we shall find that all of them, Judaism, Islam, Zoroastrianism, Buddhism, Christianity, even Confucianism, indeed claim absolute validity, but quite naïvely, and that in a very different manner in each case, the differences being illustrative of differences in their inner structure. These claims are always naïve—simple and direct. They are not the outcome of an apologetic reasoning, and the differences they exhibit in their naïve claims to absolute validity indicate the varying degree of such absolute validity as they really mean and intend within their own minds. This seemed to me to be nearly the most important point in every comparison between the religions, and the one which furnished the most searching test of the character of the dogmatic contents to be compared—contents which, in themselves, reveal so little as to the manner of their foundation in immediate religious experience.

A similar line of thought is to be found in the excellent book on *National and Universal Religions*, by the Dutch writer, Abraham Kuenen. If we make his distinction the basis of our investigation and comparison, we at once perceive that Judaism and Zoroastrianism were explicitly national religions, associated with a particular country and concerned with tasks presented by a particular type of civilisation—in the case of the Jews primarily with questions of national loyalty and national aspiration. Islam, too, is at bottom the national religion of the Arab peoples, compelling by the sword recognition of the prophetic claims of Mohammed in all the countries to which the Arab races have penetrated. Where, on the other hand, it has spread beyond the boundaries of Arabian territory, it has not as a rule attempted to convert unbelievers, but has simply maintained them as a source of revenue. And where Islam has developed great missionary activity, as, for example, in Africa and in the islands of the Malay Archipelago, it shows itself to be bound to certain conditions of civilisation which render it more readily acceptable to primitive races than Christianity, but which prove it, at the same time, to be indissolubly connected with a particular type of civilisation. Finally, where it has adopted Persian or Indian mysticism, or Greek or modern philosophy, it loses its essential character, and becomes no more than a sign and a proof of national autonomy. Confucianism and Buddhism again are rather philosophies than religions, and owe their claim to absolute validity more to the common character of thought than to belief in a specific religious revelation, whilst Confucianism is essentially a national movement and Buddhism is, as a matter of fact, bound to the conditions of life in tropical countries.

Now, the naïve claim to absolute validity made by Christianity is of quite a different kind. All limitation to a particular race or nation is excluded on principle, and this exclusion illustrates the purely human character of its religious ideal, which appeals only to the simplest, the most general, the most personal and spiritual needs of mankind. Moreover, it does not depend in any way upon human reflection or a laborious process of reasoning, but upon an overwhelming manifestation of God in the persons and lives of the great prophets. Thus it was not a theory but a life—not a social order but a power. It owes its claim to universal validity not to the correctness of its reasoning nor to the conclusiveness of its proofs, but to God's revelation of Himself in human hearts and lives. Thus the naïve claim to absolute validity of Christianity is as unique as its conception of God. It is indeed a corollary of its belief in a revelation within the depths of the soul, awakening men to a new and higher quality of life, breaking down the barriers which the sense of guilt would otherwise set up, and making a final breach with the egoism obstinately centred in the individual self. It is from this point of view that its claim to absolute validity, following as it does from the content of its religious ideal, appears to be vindicated. It possesses the highest claim to universality of all the religions, for this its claim is based upon the deepest foundations, the nature of God and of man.

Hence we may simply leave aside the question of the measure of validity possessed by the other religions. Nor need we trouble ourselves with the question of the possible further development of religion itself. It suffices that Christianity is itself a developing religion, constantly striving towards a fresh and fuller expression. We may content ourselves with acknowledging that it possesses the highest degree of validity attained among all the historical religions which we are able to examine. We shall not wish to become Jews, nor Zoroastrians, nor Mohammedans, nor again Confucianists nor Buddhists. We shall rather strive continually to bring our Christianity into harmony with the changing conditions of life, and to bring its human and divine potentialities to the fullest possible fruition. It is the loftiest and most spiritual revelation we know at all. It has the highest validity. Let that suffice.

Such was the conclusion I reached in the book which I wrote some twenty years ago, and, from the practical standpoint at least, it contains nothing that I wish to withdraw. From the point of view of theory, on the other hand, there are a number of points which I should wish to modify to-day, and these modifications are, of course, not without some practical effects.

My scruples arise from the fact that, whilst the significance for history of the concept of

Individuality impresses me more forcibly every day, I no longer believe this to be so easily reconcilable with that of supreme validity. The further investigations, especially into the history of Christianity, of which I have given the results in my *Social Doctrines* (*Die Soziallehren der christlichen Kirchen und Gruppen*, 1912), have shown me how thoroughly individual is historical Christianity after all, and how invariably its various phases and denominations have been due to varying circumstances and conditions of life. Whether you regard it as a whole or in its several forms, it is a purely historical, individual, relative phenomenon, which could, as we actually find it, only have arisen in the territory of the classical culture, and among the Latin and Germanic races. The Christianity of the Oriental peoples—the Jacobites, Nestorians, Armenians, Abyssinians—is of quite a different type, indeed even that of the Russians is a world of its own. The inference from all that is, however, that a religion, in the several forms assumed by it, always depends upon the intellectual, social, and national conditions among which it exists. On the other hand, a study of the non-Christian religions convinced me more and more that their naïve claims to absolute validity are also genuinely such.

I found Buddhism and Brahminism especially to be really humane and spiritual religions, capable of appealing in precisely the same way to the inner certitude and devotion of their followers as Christianity, though the particular character of each has been determined by the historical, geographical, and social conditions of the countries in which it has taken shape.

The subject to which I devoted most attention, however, was that of the relation of individual historical facts to standards of value within the entire domain of history in connection with the development of political, social, ethical, æsthetic, and scientific ideas. I have only lately published the results of these investigations in my new book on *The Historical Temper and its Problems* (*Der Historismus und seine Probleme*), 1922. I encountered the same difficulties in each of these provinces—they were not confined to religion. Indeed, even the validity of science and logic seemed to exhibit, under different skies and upon different soil, strong individual differences present even in their deepest and innermost rudiments. What was really common to mankind, and universally valid for it, seemed, in spite of a general kinship and capacity for mutual understanding, to be at bottom exceedingly little, and to belong more to the province of material goods than to the ideal values of civilisation.

The effect of these discoveries upon the conclusions reached in my earlier book was as follows:

The individual character of European civilisation, and of the Christian religion which is intimately connected with it, receives now much greater emphasis, whilst the somewhat rationalistic concept of validity, and specifically of *supreme validity*, falls considerably into the background. It is impossible to deny facts or to resist the decrees of fate. And it is historical facts that have welded Christianity into the closest connection with the civilisations of Greece, Rome and Northern Europe. All our thoughts and feelings are impregnated with Christian motives and Christian presuppositions; and, conversely, our whole Christianity is indissolubly bound up with elements of the ancient and modern civilisations of Europe. From being a Jewish sect Christianity has become the religion of all Europe. It stands or falls with European civilisation; whilst, on its own part, it has entirely lost its Oriental character and has become hellenised and westernised. Our European conceptions of personality and its eternal, divine right, and of progress towards a kingdom of the spirit and of God, our enormous capacity for expansion and for the interconnection of spiritual and temporal, our whole social order, our science, our art—all these rest, whether we know it or not, whether we like it or not, upon the basis of this de-orientalised Christianity.

Its primary claim to validity is thus the fact that only through it have we become what we are, and that only in it can we preserve the religious forces that we need. Apart from it we lapse either into a self-destructive titanic attitude, or into effeminate trifling, or into crude brutality. And at the same time our life is a consistent compromise as little unsatisfactory as we can manage between its lofty spirituality and our practical everyday needs—a compromise that has to be renewed at every fresh ascent and every bend of the road. This tension is characteristic of our form of human life and rouses us to many an heroic endeavour, though it may also lead us into the most terrible mendacity and crime. Thus we are, and thus we shall remain, as long as we survive. We cannot live without a religion, yet the only religion that we can endure is Christianity, for Christianity has grown up with us and has become a part of our very being.

Now, obviously we cannot remain in these matters at the level of brute fact. Christianity could not be the religion of such a highly developed racial group if it did not possess a mighty spiritual power and truth; in short, if it were not, in some degree, a manifestation of the Divine Life itself. The evidence we have for this remains essentially the same, whatever may be our theory concerning absolute validity—it is the evidence of a profound inner experience. This experience is undoubtedly the criterion of its validity, but, be it noted, only of its validity *for us*. It is God's countenance as revealed to us; it is the way in which, being what we are, we receive, and react to, the revelation of God. It is binding upon us, and it brings us deliverance. It is final and unconditional for us, because we have nothing else, and because in what we have we can recognise the accents of the divine voice.

But this does not preclude the possibility that other racial groups, living under entirely different cultural conditions, may experience their contact with the Divine Life in quite a different way, and may themselves also possess a religion which has grown up with them, and from which they cannot sever themselves so long as they remain what they are. And they may quite sincerely regard this as absolutely valid for them, and give expression to this absolute validity according to the demands of their own religious feeling. We shall, of course, assume something of this kind only among nations which have reached a relatively high stage of civilisation, and whose whole mental life has been intimately connected with their religion through a long period of discipline. We shall not assume it among the less developed races, where many religious cults are followed side by side, nor in the simple animism of heathen tribes, which is so monotonous in spite of its many variations. These territories are gradually conquered by the great world-religions which possess a real sense of their own absolute validity. But among the great spiritual religions themselves the fundamental spiritual positions which destiny has assigned to them persist in their distinctness. If we wish to determine their relative value, it is not the religions alone that we must compare, but always only the civilisations of which the religion in each case constitutes a part incapable of severance from the rest. But who will presume to make a really final pronouncement here? Only God Himself, who has determined these differences, can do that. The various racial groups can only seek to purify and enrich their experience, each within its own province and according to its own standards, and to win the weaker and less developed races for their own faith, always remembering that the religion thus adopted by another people will individualise itself anew.

The practical bearing of this new manner of thinking differs but little from that of my earlier view, or indeed from that of any theology which seeks to retain the essential basis of Christianity, and intends merely to substantiate and to interpret it. Its detailed application, however, brings to light one or two important consequences.

In the first place, it has a considerable influence upon the question of foreign missions. Missionary enterprise has always been in part simply a concomitant of the political, military, and commercial expansion of a state or nation, but in part also an outcome of the religious enthusiast's zeal for conversion. The former aspect is exceedingly important as a factor in human history, but is irrelevant in the present connection. The latter aspect, on the other hand, is intimately connected with the claim to absolute validity. But here we have to maintain, in accordance with all our conclusions hitherto, that directly religious missionary enterprise must stand in quite a different relation to the great philosophical world-religions from that in which it stands to the crude heathenism of smaller tribes. There can be always only a spiritual wrestling of missionary Christianity with the other world-religions, possibly a certain contact with them. The heathen races, on the other hand, are being morally and spiritually disintegrated by the contact with European civilisation; hence they demand a substitute from the higher religion and culture. We have a missionary duty towards these races, and our enterprise is likely to meet with success amongst them, although Christianity, be it remembered, is by no means the only religion which is taking part in this missionary campaign. Islam and Buddhism are also missionary religions. But in relation to the great world-religions we need to recognise that they are expressions of the religious consciousness corresponding to certain definite types of culture, and that it is their duty to increase in depth and purity by means of their own interior impulses, a task in which the contact with Christianity may prove helpful, to them as to us, in such processes of development from within. The great religions might indeed be described as crystallisations of the thought of great races, as these races are themselves crystallisations of the various biological and anthropological forms. There can be no conversion or transformation of one into the other, but only a measure of agreement and of mutual understanding.

The second practical consequence of my new trend of thought concerns the inner development of Christianity itself. If my theory is correct, this development is closely related to the whole spiritual and cultural development of European civilisation. True, the religious consciousness, whose object is God and eternal peace, is less exposed to restlessness and change than are the purely temporal constituents of the movement; hence it has become institutionalised in the various large denominations which, because of these internal reasons, constitute the most conservative element in the life of Europe. Nevertheless, Christianity is drawn into the stream of spiritual development even within the Churches, and still more outside and beyond them, in the free speculation of literature and philosophy. Moreover, it contains, like all the world-religions, and perhaps more than any other world-religion, the impulse and the power to a continual self-purification and self-deepening, for it has been assigned to that Spirit which shall lead men into all truth, and which seeks its fulfilment in the coming of the Kingdom of God ; and again, because it has been bound up from the first with all the intellectual forces of Hellenism.

Under these circumstances the course of its development is unpredictable, for it is capable of assuming always new individualisations. A new era in the world's history is beginning for it at this moment. It has to ally itself anew to a new conception of nature, a new social order, and a profound interior transformation of the spiritual outlook, and has to bring to the suffering world a new peace and a new brotherhood. How this can be accomplished it is not for me to say here; indeed, the answer is as yet very far from clear. All that is certain is that Christianity is at a critical moment of its further development, and that very bold and far-reaching changes are necessary, transcending anything that has yet been achieved by any denomination. I have, in this respect, become more and more radical and super-denominational, whilst, at the same time, I have come more and more to regard the specific kernel of religion as a unique and independent source of life and power.

Can we, then, discover no common goal of religion, nothing at all that is absolute, in the objective sense of constituting a common standard for mankind? Instinctive conviction makes us reluctant to admit such a sceptical conclusion, and it will especially be combated on the ground of the reality of the subjective validities which we have discovered. These are not simply illusions or the products of human vanity. They are products of the impulse towards absolute objective truth, and take effect in the practical sphere under constant critical self-purification and effort at self-improvement. I have already drawn attention to this fact in my earlier work. I only wish to emphasise now more strongly than I did then that this synthesis cannot as yet be already attained in any one of the historical religions, but that they all are tending in the same direction, and that all seem impelled by an inner force to strive upward towards some unknown final height, where alone the ultimate unity and the final objective validity can lie. And, as all religion has thus a common goal in the Unknown, the Future, perchance in the Beyond, so too it has a common ground in the Divine Spirit ever pressing the finite mind onward towards further light and fuller consciousness, a Spirit Which indwells the finite spirit, and Whose ultimate union with it is the purpose of the whole many-sided process.

Between these two poles, however,—the divine Source and the divine Goal—lie all the individual differentiations of race and civilisation, and, with them also, the individual differences of the great, comprehensive religions. There may be mutual understanding between them, if they are willing to renounce those sorry things, self-will and the spirit of violent domination. If each strives to fulfil its own highest potentialities, and allows itself to be influenced therein by the similar striving of the rest, they may approach and find contact with each other. Some striking examples of such contact are recorded in Canon Streeter's *The Sadhu*, and in a book called *On the Verge of the Primitive Forest*, by the Alsatian physician and writer on the philosophy of religion, Albert Schweitzer. But, so far as human eye can penetrate into the future, it would seem probable that the great revelations to the various civilisations will remain distinct, in spite of a little shifting of their several territories at the fringes, and that the question of their several relative values will never be capable of objective determination, since every proof thereof will presuppose the special characteristics of the civilisation in which it arises. The conception of personality itself is, for instance, different in the east and in the west, hence arguments starting from it will lead to different conclusions in the two cases. Yet there is no other concept which could furnish a basis for argument concerning practical values and truths save this concept of personality, which is always itself already one of the fundamental positions of the several religions, and is determined by them according to these respective general attitudes of theirs.

This is what I wish to say in modification of my former theories. I hope you feel that I am not speaking in any spirit of scepticism or uncertainty. A truth which, in the first instance, is *a truth for us* does not cease, because of this, to be very Truth and Life. What we learn daily through our love for our fellow-men, viz. that they are independent beings with standards of their own, we ought also to be able to learn through our love for mankind as a whole—that here too there exist autonomous civilisations with standards of their own. This does not exclude rivalry, but it must be a rivalry for the attainment of interior purity and clearness of vision. If each racial group strives to develop its own highest potentialities, we may hope to come nearer to one another. This applies to the great world-religions, but it also applies to the various religious denominations, and to individuals in their intercourse with one another. In our earthly experience the Divine Life is not One, but Many. But to apprehend the One in the Many constitutes the special character of love.

Section II

ETHIK UND GESCHICHTSPHILOSOPHIE

Three Lectures written for delivery to the Advanced Students in Theology of the University of London in March 1923.

Section II

ETHICS AND THE PHILOSOPHY OF HISTORY

Three Lectures translated by various hands.

1

DIE PERSÖNLICHKEITS—UND GEWISSENSMORAL

I

THE MORALITY OF THE PERSONALITY AND OF THE CONSCIENCE

Translated by Baron F. von Hügel *and* Principal Ernest Barker.

1
THE MORALITY OF THE PERSONALITY AND OF THE CONSCIENCE

You have done me the high honour of inviting me to deliver three lectures under the auspices of your famous University, and I accept the invitation with pride and gratitude. I can best show my pride and my gratitude by choosing a theme which is the very centre of all my thought at the present time, and gives me the opportunity of offering myself, with the practical and theoretical views which are of paramount importance for my own mind, to your friendly criticism.

This central theme concerns the relation between the endless movement of the stream of historical life and the need of the human mind to limit and to shape it by means of fixed standards. This is a question which arose for me in my early adult life in the domain of religious philosophy and theology, where not only historical and philosophical criticism, but, above all, the historical entanglements and the historical variability of Christianity so greatly increase the difficulty of finding firm principles for the living present. But the question very soon proved itself to be much more general than this. The same problem exists for the sum of all standards in general, and not only for the standards of the religious life in particular. In the State, in Society and in Economics, and also in Science and in Art, the same problem reappears. The so-called natural standards are in no way more firmly fixed than the standards which we call supernatural ; and all attempts to fix the one from the side of the other are illusory, from whichever side we may care to start our labour. And, over and above all this, the entire question is by no means the raising of a merely personal problem ; it is a problem brought home to us by the entire situation of our times. It is the general mind of our times which finds itself shaken to its depths and in a state of change in almost every direction ; and all this commotion is accompanied throughout by an almost alarming perspicacity in historical reflection and comparison. It is due to this position of affairs that considerations of an historical-philosophical kind again play the part to-day which they did before and after the French Revolution—in the age of Rousseau, Voltaire, and Herder, and again in the age of Hegel and of Comte.

Meanwhile, however, the historical horizon has become very much wider both in space and in time, and our knowledge of the past has become much more differentiated, more exact, and more objective. Our contemporary literature is full of comparative and evolutionary considerations varying from primitive man in the Ice Age down to the most modern European and Asiatic civilisation, and from Australia and Central Africa to Europe, America, and Eastern Asia. The immense variety and movement apparent in this gigantic body of material for our historical comparisons at first profoundly interested us and broadened our minds, so long as it all could be easily comprised within the series of an evolutionary progress, and so long as our own position, as the summit of this progress, remained beyond doubt. But the more difficult the construction of such an evolutionary series finally became, in the increasing exactitude of research, and the more our own proud present revealed alarming cleavages and gaps, the more did the problem I have attempted to indicate obtrude itself, both theoretically and practically, in a manner which compelled attention and evoked anxiety. The idea of a humane European order, expressing itself in the organisation of the states and the societies appertaining to it, was dissolved by criticism, and gave way to all sorts of plans for the distant future, or to pessimism, or to purely materialist appreciation of interests which can only be realised by violence. Nietzsche spoke of the irruption of European nihilism, and the great Russian novelists turned away with horror from the West in its decomposition, the essence of which they conceived to be Criticism, Psychology, Evolution, and finally despair of what is called Progress.

Behind all this lie the problems of the Philosophy of History—the problems of controlling and dominating the immense stream of historical life, a stream which grows continually more rapid and more extended, and not merely of constructing theoretically its successive stages and its laws of movement. But this means, in other words, that History requires us to come to grips with the idea of an abiding system of values which shall give us our standards, even though every such system seems always to be undermined and washed away by this stream. But such a system of values is nothing else than what we call, in other words, the system of Ethics. Hence the great question is: what is the rôle and the significance of the system of Ethics for the great task of controlling and damming the historical movement, which, in itself, is simply boundless? And this is the question on which I should like to speak in these three lectures.

I have everywhere assumed in my hearers a knowledge of the nature of modern historico-critical inquiry, and a sense of the consequences and dangers pertaining to such inquiry. This is perhaps, here in England, less intensively at work than it is amongst us on the Continent; and yet here also, as the religious, political, and social unrests and argumentations show, it is sufficiently strong not to find itself overcome any longer by simple appeals to tradition, custom, and political propriety. At bottom we are all, in our every fibre, aware of Historical Relativism; and there is no need, therefore, of any closer elucidation of its origin, nature, and effect. The most living problem of actual life consists in the question whether, and how far, a conceptually assured and clarified Ethic can master and limit this historical Relativism.

Yet we must admit that, in the domain of Ethics, in its present form, the same problems which exist elsewhere recur in somewhat different shapes ; and, indeed, further problems appear which arise from the inner nature and difficulty of the ethical idea itself.

The entire domain of the ethical standards has itself been drawn, by Modern Psychology, by historical Relativism, and by Evolutionism, into the flow of things, and been made part and parcel of this Historicism. The impulse of modern-minded men, apparently all-powerful, towards simplification and deductions of a highly monistic type, has led to the derivation of the ethical standards themselves from instincts which are either pre-ethical or not yet ethical in character, just as Darwinism, enlarged into a philosophy, has attempted to derive apparently firm and purposive forms from crossings between the purposeless and accidental. After David Hume and Adam Smith had begun to explain the origin of the illusion of objective moral commands in a suggestive and acute manner, the proofs furnished by Sociology of the dependence of the ethical standards on the varying needs of society and the relations between Capital and Labour seemed definitely to complete this monistic explanation and derivation. This was the origin of Utilitarianism and Ethical Empiricism, in its numerous forms, though in the end it ceased to be able to furnish a foundation for any abiding system of Morality, and led to a general moral scepticism or to a mere Practicism or Pragmatism.

But it is not these questions which I would here consider. These questions stand or fall with the general theory of a Monistic Empiricism, which has taken it into its head to reduce all standards to accidents of the psychological mechanism, and to trace back all the imperative laws of first principles to natural, psychological, or psycho-physical laws of the stream of consciousness, and this though in all other possible respects the world remains full of dualisms and pluralisms. Against this Monistic Empiricism we can but advance the old line of thought which Plato already advanced against the Sophists and Naturalists—a line of thought formulated afresh in modern times, more particularly by Kant, but already advanced before his time, in England by the school of Reid against the school of Hume and in France by Descartes against the Sceptics. Logically all moral, juristic, and æsthetic principles are and remain principles which oppose themselves to the flow of the psychological determinist mechanism, and derive their right and their necessity from their significance and content, quite independently of their origin in the psychological concatenation. Not the "how?" of their genesis but the "that" of their objectively significant contents and of their logical connections is here decisive. This applies to all the domains concerned with standards, and therefore to the moral domain also. How the stream of consciousness can make such a continuous severance of itself into genetically explicable mechanisms and principles which themselves furnish their authority by their objectively significant contents—that is a further question, but it can alter nothing in the actual facts, which are entirely clear and decisive for the very possibility of all thinking.

It is not at this point that the problem lies. It lies in the fact that the principles which arise in this way are still also subject on their part to deep historical changes, and that they themselves are anything but simple, but, on the contrary, full of an interior tension and distinctly complex. The question of the origin of this fact would lead us too far into the further question of the interior developments of the spirit and all its incursions into the mere psychic life; but that is a metaphysical question and one which is perhaps incapable of explanation. I desire here to confine myself simply to the position of the facts as they lie before us; to accept the historical conditionality and complexity of the standards simply as a fact; and to analyse it only with the object of discovering how, in these circumstances, the principle which is at the same time a standard can nevertheless be attained for any and every present. And further I would desire, in following this procedure, to return from the broad and great conception of the standard principles in general to the particular ethical principles which were described in the beginning. The comparison of these ethical principles with the logical principles in which the autonomous independence of the postulate attains its greatest clearness is, after all, only a comparison. And although Kant has been particularly successful in making clear the ethical principles by means of this comparison, he has nevertheless pushed this comparison too far and approximated the ethical too closely to the logical. In reality we must see to it that, after this comparison has rendered all the services of which it is capable for the cognition of the autonomy which also belongs to the ethical, our attention is turned to the ethical phenomenon in its peculiarity.

Now the peculiarity of the ethical phenomenon consists in a quite extraordinary complexity of the ethical consciousness, the standards of which flow together from very different sources and directions, and the tensions within which, produced by these very differences, have always to be included together anew in a single final result. True, the logical also is not as simple and as free from tension as it appears to the man in the street. General Formal Logic, the Empirical Logic of the Sciences of Nature, and finally the Logic of Philosophy which brings the Many and their contradictions to unity, all arise from different sources and different directions of thought; and the drawing of them all together into a unity of outlook forms the eternal and special difficulty of all Philosophy. But these divisions of logical thought have nothing to do with the divisions within ethical thought, and they do not of themselves explain the complexities of the latter. In any case this is true for the facts which lie immediately to hand—facts which we have to analyse by a direct confrontation. If we follow this procedure, the decisive conclusion is the complexity of the Ethical Consciousness. This complexity is confirmed by every glance at experience and at historical reality; it is the real reason why a Science of Ethics is so immensely difficult, and why it has led less than all the other philosophical sciences, with the possible exception of Æsthetics, to abiding results and to general recognition. It is what we find mirrored, too, in the oppositions and contradictions between the ethical systems themselves ; for they by no means spring only from a distinction between the empirical and the categorical derivation of the ethical standards, but arise quite as much from the internal objective tensions and complexities of Ethical Thought itself. True, this second side of the ethical problem has always attracted less notice than the first, which resounds in almost the entire literature of Ethics, from the time of the Greeks down to ourselves. This springs spontaneously from the natural impulse of Ethics to reach a single form of standard. But in itself the second series of differences is the more important, and in reality it lies far more at the root of the differences between the historical systems of Ethics, though it must be confessed that this has seldom been apprehended by their exponents.

Let us first attempt to draw out of this complex fabric the thread which lies most clearly before our eyes and promises to lead us more securely than any other to our end, to a universal and objective determination of the ethical standard.

This thread consists in the determinations of what we call Conscience; in the general moral demands of the traditional doctrine of the virtues and the duties; in the demands of personal moral dignity, of strength of character and self-conquest on the one hand, and of justice, benevolence, and public spirit on the other. We have thus to do with the old virtues, elaborated by the Socratic school and more precisely fixed by the Stoics, which later, under the influence of Christianity, appear more as divine demands and hence as duties. These are, in reality, the general formal standards which proceed from the nature of the Moral Consciousness. But if we are determined to deduce them more precisely from this consciousness, we shall not be able, like the most severe of the modern ethical thinkers, to deduce them simply from the universality and objectivity of the Moral Reason, or only and immediately from the conception of a categorical imperative. We shall have to consider that Ethics is an action; that all action is a realisation of ends; and, therefore, that the unity of Ethics too can only be deduced from the end, as indeed even Kant finally realised in some of his incidental and auxiliary thinking. Now, the end of moral action which first appears in an obvious manner is the attainment and the defence of a free personality, which has its foundations in itself and possesses a certain unity of its own. The idea of personality is the decisive idea. Out of the flux and confusion of the life of the instincts, the unity and compactness of personality has first to be created and acquired.

No man is born a personality; everyone has first to make himself into a personality by obedience towards another instinct, which leads to unity and homogeneity. Freedom and creation constitute the secret of personality, but this self-creation of personality is, of course, no absolute creation in us finite creatures who emerge from the stream of life and of consciousness. It is a creation which takes place in obedience and in devotion to an attraction towards emancipation from merely natural and accidental determination—an attraction to the imperative "ought" which is analogous to the attraction towards logical truth and correctness, and arises, like the latter, from the deeper spiritual levels of our being. So far it is a purely formal aim of independence from mere fate, and of self-determination from within, through the ideal of an internal unity and clarity of our being, which ought to be, and obliges us. It is a distinct and independent question what are to be the concrete single ends by which certain qualities are to be acquired that will strengthen and bring out the general independence. Our further inquiry will have to occupy itself with this further question, and it is from this point of view that the complexity of Ethics will appear in its fullest light. Hitherto this second question has not appeared upon our horizon; but, as the price for this simplicity of outlook, we have only to do with the purely formal end, with the unity, centrality, homogeneity, consistency, and purity of intention of the personality, all considered as characteristics which ought to exist.

From this end or aim which ought to exist the particular demands of Ethics can be derived without difficulty as soon as we consider that, in the first place, this personality has to develop itself in a double direction, in a particular demeanour towards itself, and in a particular demeanour towards its neighbour; and that, in the second place, the characteristic of personality applies as a demand made not only of single men but also of communities, so that not only individual but also corporate personalities are required. But the demands, purely formal as they are in their nature, which arise in these several directions, can attain so great an independence as single demands that it is possible to forget, in consequence, the connection of them all with the fundamental end contained in the sense of obligation generally, and again the fact that this general end is intrinsically related to a concrete cultural subject-matter in which it has to find the stuff for its activity. Such forgetfulness has often enough occurred, both practically and theoretically; and whenever it occurs the particular commandments each appear as something absolute, as something which is its own guarantee, whilst, in reality, they are only that through their connection with the general imperative on the one hand and with the particular subject-matter of action on the other.

As regards the dependence of the particular commandments upon the general commandment, ethical demeanour divides itself, in consequence of this connection, into duties towards oneself and duties towards one's neighbour, as traditional morality, formally perhaps somewhat offensively, but quite rightly as concerns the content, formulates its character. Action in regard to our own self demands first of all strict veracity or unison with oneself, the energy and the strength of character which expresses itself in an inter-connected moral life, and the disposition which is directed to inner moral values in contradiction to all and every eudaemonism: in a word, the elaboration and the persistent defence of moral dignity. In regard to one's neighbour, moral action aims at the conception and the treatment of this neighbour as not only a means but, at the same time, an end in himself, who, precisely like ourselves, possesses or is called to the dignity of a human being. In this celebrated Kantian phrase, all that is essential is already expressed. In it is contained more especially the demand of justice—the justice which contemplates life and things, not only from its own standpoint, but also from the standpoint of other men, and, at the same time, is directed towards the recognition and the advancement of the moral dignity of the neighbour. This recognition is the justice which everywhere establishes a certain proportion, corresponding to the whole ethical value of the several persons, and allots their place in it according to the circumstances —to honour or loyal obedience, to gratitude or to blame, to resistance or to the influence of the educator. In so far as this justice is joy in the moral dignity of one's neighbour, or is education and aid brought to some incipient moral worth, it becomes kindness ; and from this connection with justice even kindness and benevolence become a duty, which persists so long as we are not obliged to convince ourselves of the opposite and of the impossibility of improving our neighbour. All further moral theories and lists of the virtues and the duties, such as are dear to ancient and modern moralists, are only further elaborations of these simple fundamental ideas, and may be left untouched here.

As concerns the second kind of personality, the group, all the determinations of the morality of solidarity belong to it—a morality in which the natural consciousness of the group is transfigured into an ethically founded devotion to a moral, super-individual Whole. And in such a transfiguration it is, in the first instance, presupposed that this Whole itself— this family, tribe, class, corporation, nation, humanity—is no mere result of blood, or of nature, or of instincts and habits, but needs to be considered and felt as a community in certain ethical values, a community which ought to be ; it is presupposed, in a word, that these several Wholes should not only be considered to exist, but should also really exist, as Wholes. The group, starting from its natural basis, is thus to develop into a special moral community through the union and inter-connection of its members; and the members are to feel their devotion to this community, not merely as an instinct of nature or of habit, but as a duty in which the individual grows to a height above himself, even to the sacrifice of himself for the Whole when that becomes necessary. We have here the overcoming of the selfishness of the group, a selfishness which is in no way more venerable, though it is certainly more natural, than the selfishness of the individual; it is the overcoming of the herd-instinct or the mere co-operation of interests. Such a transfiguration is not possible without a continuous criticism of the unity of the group and a continuous moral ennobling of it. Nor is it possible, again, to find the justification for the sacrifice and renunciation which are thus required in the advantage which the individual is to gain thereby; it can only be found in the obligation of the Whole to purity and dignity.

But wherein the ethical value of the group itself consists, and how it can be ennobled and spiritualised from within itself—that is still another question, which cannot yet be answered on the basis of these purely formal presuppositions, and leads to further ethical questions which must be answered in the next lecture. At this point we need only add that the same rules apply to the relations of the groups, or collective personalities, towards each other, as apply to the relations of single persons with one another. Moral regulation is certainly much more difficult of accomplishment for a group than it is for individuals, because the complexity of the relations and the distribution of responsibility are greater, and indeed the moralising of the group in general is very much more difficult than the moralising of individual men; but in principle we have to do with the same demands of justice and of kindness, of recognition and of education, of respect and of support. At this point the moral demand rises to the ideal of Humanity—of a community of all mankind in which the national groups are morally bound to each other and depend upon each other in the same way as the single social groups within the several nations. This is what constitutes the moral conception or ideal of Humanity, which is something different from the anthropological or geographical conception of the populations of the globe and the presumable relationship in blood of all creatures that bear the face of man. All these demands which are thus applied to group personalities are necessary consequences of the fundamental principle of Formal Ethics, as soon as this principle comes to be pressed to its last consequences. Hence these doctrines continually recur in all ethical systems as the doctrines of Humanity, of the Love of Mankind, of International Justice, of the Rights of Man, and of Progress. Ever since the age of the Stoics extended the horizon of Ethics in principle beyond the national range, these doctrines have really constituted moral demands of a universal validity, which have passed into Christian ideas of the morality of peoples and, again, into modern ideas of humanity and of progress towards moral purification and unity. But we have always to bear in mind that it is not simply men and groups, as so many natural beings, with which we have to do, but men and groups as rational beings and as personalities which have first to produce themselves by free acts of determination.

Is it, then, possible, and may we expect, that the historical stream of life can be defined and shaped for us in the light of these ideas which follow from the formal nature of moral obligation? Many moralists demand and maintain it: they postulate only, as its condition, that necessary self-conquest and that indispensable radicalism by which mere Nature and her instinctive confused egoism must be brought under the yoke. Others regard it as impossible ; and they accordingly reject in their entirety the very assumptions of such a mental structure, which is contradicted, as they believe, by the totally different character of the actual process of reality.

It cannot be denied that the relation of these mental structures to actual history presents a difficult problem.

In the first place, we have to put to ourselves the question, " Do these demands, which spring from the timeless nature of obligation or reason, and are therefore perfectly objective, universal, and identical with reason itself—do they really and actually appear in history itself so universally and originally as on this theory they are bound to do ? " In facing this question we can leave entirely out of account the extent of their realisation, and even the possibility or impossibility of their realisation ; but in any case they must be universally diffused as demands (which, whether realised or no, are actually made).

An answer to the question would carry us far into evolutionary and sociological investigations, and especially into extremely difficult investigations of primitive man and his possible survivals and analogies. Such investigations are impossible in this connection; and they are also unnecessary. Reason, and the idea of personality—which is closely connected with reason—is still in process of growth, disengaging itself everywhere, even yet, from its natural basis; climbing upward from the preparatory stage of the natural life of instinct; and seeking to deliver itself from that stage, as it recognises its opposition to it, in order to achieve its own independence. So far as its content is concerned, it is a matter of indifference when, where, and how this is done. This content, whenever it has grasped its own independence, proceeds to grow by its own purely rational laws, and ceases to be determined by psychological factors. Such a "conversion" or "break through" must have happened in innumerable cases and places; and even to-day, in spite of all tradition and education, it must constantly happen afresh whenever an independent moral person, single or collective, is to burst its sheath. Even in regard to the primitive, investigation is steadily showing, with an ever-growing force, that moral demands of this order have actually developed themselves everywhere, in a greater or less degree of purity and perfection, to constitute the internal morality of exclusive groups. Regard for character, honesty, self-control, justice, and benevolence is a quality which naturally grows first within narrow groups, depending on personal intercourse and ready community of sentiment; and it is mixed with every possible religious and sociological motive. It is only in such groups that we find dominant that atmosphere of mutual confidence in which these moral demands can grow and be obeyed. Externally, and in the struggle of groups, there reigns an atmosphere of mistrust, in which, in the main, it is only the morality of courage, of group-solidarity, and, at best, of fidelity to engagements which can arise. Only when groups are very highly developed are they able to knit bonds of union which transcend the antagonism of groups, nations, and races—bonds which are woven of the stuff of pure humanity, and made by the extension of internal to international morality. Here again, when this point has been reached, the virtues and the duties already mentioned are constantly reappearing as decisive. Even yet, however, it is not so much groups themselves as it is particular individuals, of an advanced thought and an inward enlightenment, who are united and controlled by this morality of personality. Even to-day groups still remain, for the most part, in an atmosphere of mistrust and struggle for existence, according to the sociological law that masses find their bond of cohesion more readily in material interests and elementary passions than in the higher spiritual purposes and values. This defect has been to some extent remedied, but it has by no means been removed, by the great universal religions, by scientific enlightenment, by the interchange of philosophic thought, and by humanised international law. In the last few years we have ourselves had tragic experience of its existence.

I conclude that it is not the actual diffusion, or non-diffusion, of this universal morality which is the essential problem; it is the question of its real practicability. Now this morality is always, to begin with, a controlling and conquering of mere nature, from which it springs, but with which it struggles. In its essence it is a perpetual struggle and a perpetual creation. The very conception of this morality means that it can never be simply victorious. Victory would be the end of struggle and freedom: it would be the absolute and effortless necessity of the good and of reason; and that is something which we cannot picture to ourselves. And this is the reason why the religious always

THE MORALITY OF CONSCIENCE 63

transcends the moral; why the highest ideal is elevated to an incomprehensible other-world of Love or to a passionless supra-moral peace of the spirit. But it is not only this essential element of struggle in all moral life which makes it impossible to disengage the moral from its admixture of natural instincts and natural needs, and which must always prevent its full realisation. There is another reason. These instincts and needs have, and they continue to maintain, their own independent justification in the nature of man, as it struggles for room, for food, for life, for more life; and in man's earthly life they can never be completely excluded or rationally organised. The conflict between Nature and Morality, between the demands of subsistence and the shaping of moral personality, can never be completely solved. The most advanced theories which assume such a solution—the theories of communism and socialism—are consequently bound to assume two miracles: the miracle of a technique which puts Nature completely and adequately at the service of man, and which must include, as part of itself, the technique of a proper regulation of the numbers of the population; and the miracle of a new education, which enthrones Reason and Morality, alike in the relations of individuals and of groups, completely above the natural turmoil of instincts and the tendency towards the struggle for existence. And both of these miracles are impossible even for the boldest of hopes. The practical attempts at the realisation of such ideals have hitherto always shown that provision for natural necessities cannot be organised in this fashion; that technique fails utterly, and mass-starvation begins; that the tendency towards the struggle for existence must necessarily be diverted to some external outlet; and that fresh wars thus arise out of the gospel of peace. That is the lesson both of the French and Russian Revolutions.

In these circumstances there is no hope at all left for the realisation of the moral idea of humanity by finally and completely damming and canalising the stream of historical life through a morality which is timelessly valid and transcends history. Struggle remains to all eternity—struggle and yet again struggle—as the lot of the moral here on earth. Man is, and always will be, at once a natural and a rational being. Reconciliation can only be attained by a compromise which has always to be made afresh—a compromise which every agent must seek on his own account and at his own peril; a compromise which must always be especially difficult and involved in politics

THE MORALITY OF CONSCIENCE

and the dealings of States with one another. The only possible line of action must be that of always realising ethical purposes *as far as possible* ; of enlisting in their services, in given circumstances, powerful natural instincts ; and, in other circumstances, of leaving free play to natural forces which we cannot alter, and which perhaps we can only hope to capture again afterwards. What gives responsibility and ethical quality to our actions is just that, in a given situation, we undertake to find the right way *to the best of our knowledge and conscience*, and that we voluntarily make ourselves answerable for solving the conflict between Nature and Reason. The conformity of the moral with conviction, emphasised by Kant in his excessively idealistic Rationalism, does not consist in the pure intention of reasonableness —that may be present, and yet we may leave the actual process of action to take care of itself, and warm ourselves at our own virtue— but in the will to responsibility and decision, where the compromise between Nature and Reason is struck according to the circumstances of the moment. This is the goodwill which is in question, and not the abstract obedience to reason of the Stoics—

> Si fractus illabatur orbis
> Impavidum ferient ruinae.

There are certainly cases in which any compromise would be immoral. But they are rare ; and they always belong to the sphere of private and personal life. From the particularly complicated relations of public life it has never been possible to eliminate compromise utterly.

If this be the case, our main question in regard to the regulation of historic life by this morality can no longer be simply answered by a Yes or No. Historical Relativism can and must be limited from this point of view. It does not lead, and the knowledge of it does not lead, to a fundamental Amoralism. But the act of limitation itself is always and in every case an act which differs according to situation and circumstances, maturity of development and difficulties of life. It is a relative act, which only realises absolute standards as far as possible, and bears in its bosom its own absolute quality only in the form of decision by the personal conscience and resolution. In this act of resolution account ought to be taken of the moral laws to the fullest possible extent. We must not make it easy or comfortable for ourselves ; and in this respect an advance may very well be both possible and desirable for humanity. In the act of decision we may thus certainly trace a factor of fundamental definition and precision of direction, but not a timeless, eternally valid, abstract programme, in the light of which, at any point, on the assumption of goodwill, the problem of historical perplexities can be solved, or which, again, as the final triumph of progress, can, in any conceivable future, perfectly organise the whole of humanity.

This serious recognition must be opposed to all moralising abstraction about the philosophy of history. Even in this sphere, where we are dealing with the most universal, the most abstract, and the clearest factors of the ethical consciousness, we must confess that there is no possibility of any limitation of the historical stream of life which is finally valid. Limitation in this direction is much more readily possible for individuals than for groups, and even then the limitation remains an act of compromise, which is one with conscience. It is not for nothing that religion, which everywhere transcends all morality, teaches us that the pure will and devotion to an ideal world is sufficient for righteousness, and that life itself remains sinful—a mixture, that is to say, of nature and the divine life. Justification by faith is only a specifically religious expression for this universal relation of things. It is not for nothing that the religious idea places the individual, his decision and his salvation, in the foreground. He alone transcends history; and the inward union of the devout with one another is a heavenly object of longing or a monastic order, while it is only the ever-recurring mixture of light and darkness which suits earthly history. The kingdom of God, just because it transcends history, cannot limit or shape history. Earthly history remains the foundation and the presupposition of the final personal decision and sanctification; but in itself it goes on its way as a mixture of reason and natural instinct, and it can never be bound in any bonds except in a relative degree and for a temporary space.

2
DIE ETHIK DER KULTURWERTE

2

THE ETHICS OF THE CULTURAL VALUES

Translated by Dr. Maximilian A. Mügge (*Göttingen*) *and* Miss Doran.

Carefully revised by Principal Barker *and* Baron Hügel.

One of the collaborators at the translations here given objected to " cultural values " as not pure English and proposed instead " the values of civilisation." Another scholar friend considered " cultural values " to be sufficiently pure English and to sound strange in English ears only because we have not yet come to think of the things betokened by the phrase from the point of view of those who coined it elsewhere ; and, again, that " civilisation " is a wider term than " culture." Principal Barker *has persuaded me to retain " cultural values," but to append this explanatory note to its first deliberate introduction.*

F. v. H.

2
THE ETHICS OF CULTURAL VALUES

THE morality of personality and conscience, which differentiates into a series of precepts and blends together again in one firm thread, is only one, if it is the most conspicuous, of the threads in the rich fabric which the ethical consciousness presents. At the same time it is the one and only thread which guides us into the realm of standards beyond the reach of time or history, though, whenever these standards are practically applied, it is immediately lost again in bewildering complications, historically and individually conditioned by the particular situation.

But the ethical consciousness also presents to us at the same time an entirely different series of factors, which in traditional ethics are known as Goods or Ends, and are to-day preferably designated as Values, or, more precisely, as Cultural Values. The essence of these values is that they are obligatory values or objective ends—that is to say, actual values of a universal, more than accidental and more than individual validity, for the attainment of which we make it a duty of ourselves and of others to strive. Here again there is thus an advance beyond the accidental turmoil of psychologically explicable needs and instincts, and above the compulsory ties and the utilities of sociological unions. These cultural values are Goods and Ends of action, and thus they partake of that quality of value or pleasure without which no action can ever be set in motion. This is also true of the morality of personality and conscience, which is similarly moved to action by a value or end—the intrinsic value of the free self-controlling personality and the free spiritual-ethical complex. From any mere Eudæmonism, understanding this term in its strict and only applicable meaning, both of these moralities remain distinguished by their freedom from accidental and material cravings for the mere means of supporting life and enhancing its pleasures—the term "life" here being understood in its strictly literal application to the natural animal instincts.

In the history of ethics from the Greeks onwards the ethic of social values was from the beginning the more strongly emphasised, and remained in the first instance blended with the morality of conscience. Greek philosophy in its essence conceived of the spiritual world as artistically self-evident and closely united with the physical world ; though, at the same time, it regarded the Beautiful as the Good—that is to say, as what ought to be. The motives still blended in Greek thought were only separated at a later date, under the influence of Christianity and the less sensuous mode of thought of the northern races. The famous Platonic list of the virtues embodies in Andreia and Sophrosyne the morality of conscience ; in Sophia the perception of the systems of ethical and cultural values or ideas, so far as they were current among the Greeks in their close union of the spiritual with the physical ; and in Dikaiosyne the harmonious organisation of these various duties and values within the Polis, or ideal Greek state and society.

The later development of scientific ethics divided these elements more sharply. The ethical system of the Stoics clearly elaborated the morality of conscience and the community of mankind, though we have to admit that it remained closely intertwined with the mere natural striving for self-affirmation as a law of Nature. Roman Stoicism, like Jewish and Christian ethics, founded the morality of conscience on the Divine Will, and divided it even more deeply and fundamentally from the natural egoistical sensuous life of instinct; and it is thus that the system of thought, which holds sway to the present time in this field, has in the main been attained. Neoplatonism, the second great system of the later period of classical history, adhered more closely to the theory of moral Goods or Values, and derived such Goods from the ascending of the soul above the sensuous to the spiritual and finally to reunion with the Godhead. Hence was derived a scale, ascending from the goods of civic-political-social life to the goods of the intellectual life in the spheres of science, art, and the philosophy of religion—a scale which remained in the form of a distinction between *iustitia civilis* and *justitia spiritualis* until far into Christian times, and was especially of the first importance to the teachers of the Reformation. St. Augustine, and the ethical writers of the Middle Ages after him, connected the *lex naturae* of the Stoics, which since the time of Philo had been identified with the Decalogue of Moses, with the Neoplatonic theory of the moral goods or values, bringing the various goods, short of the *summum bonum* of the *fruitio Dei*, under the rubric of *uti, non frui*, and so depriving of their proper ethical character the

THE ETHICS OF CULTURAL VALUES

goods which belong to the world of our earthly existence.

From the time of the Renaissance the threads which had hitherto been so closely united became divergent. One school follows predominantly, if not exclusively, the morality of conscience, developing it, as Locke does, psychologically and evolutionarily from the striving after pleasure, or, like Kant, making it proceed from the basis of rational postulate which is Pure Theoretical Reason. Another school follows the theory of moral goods or values, and, in the spirit of the Renaissance, brings into greater prominence the " values " of Science, as did Spinoza and Leibniz, or the " values " of Art, as did Giordano Bruno and Shaftesbury, combining Religion closely with both of these groups of values. German Idealism, originating in the teaching of Leibniz, Kant, and the great German poetry, proceeded, in the work of Schleiermacher and Hegel, to elaborate this theory of moral goods or values into the attainment of self-consciousness by a growing Reason which, in the very process of growth, finds its own comprehension of itself. From this Reason Hegel deduced a system of moral goods or values, which men dreamed of realising in a State animated by a new spirit, and, above all, in the curriculum of the new German Universities. The thought of Western Europe, on the other hand, with its inclination towards a monistic Empiricism, endeavoured to derive these moral goods or values from the needs and the development of the community, and formed a system of values based upon sociological conditions, which was expounded with great ingenuity and learning by Comte and Herbert Spencer.

To pursue the history of Ethics in further detail is unnecessary. What matters is that we should recognise clearly, in the first place, that it shows from the earliest stages a divergence in the two main directions which we have indicated, and secondly, that there is no relation of mutual exclusion, but rather one of mutual connection, between the two. The two together constitute the sphere of Ethics in its entirety, though it is true that the establishment of a connection between them remains for the most part a very confused or casual affair. Such a connection has been established by facts and by life itself rather than by theory ; and it has only been attained at all in theory by dint of elaborate joinery or else of violent assertions. The strong influence of the theological dogmas of Authority, and of the exceedingly complicated theological association of the highest religious Good with Moral Dignity, has caused an additional confusion of theories; whether we regard the positive influence of Theology or the attempts of its enemies to escape from its influence. The essential thing is, that we are concerned with two different spheres of the moral consciousness. It is to be desired that the two spheres should also be distinguished terminologically. There is an advantage here in adopting the practice of many thinkers, who designate the first sphere, that of the commands of conscience, as Morals in its strict and essential significance, and the other, that of the cultural values, as Ethics in the wider Greek sense of the term; and indeed these terms may very well supersede the old clumsy designations of "The Theory of Virtues and Duties" on the one hand, and of "The Theory of Moral Goods" on the other. Other thinkers now prefer to recognise a distinction between the ethic of the commandments and the ethic of the cultural values; and there is this advantage in such nomenclature, that the term Ethics is retained as the general concept for both spheres.

Of more importance than this terminological clarification, which in the long run is always of a somewhat arbitrary nature, and is continually struggling with the laxities and the element of idiom in ordinary speech, is a genuine insight into the necessity of such a distinction and especially into the reaction of these two spheres upon one another. Some allusion had naturally to be made to this matter before in our analysis of the morality of conscience. It can hardly be too frequently emphasised that in such morality the aim always before the mind is purely formal: it is the self-sufficiency of a free, self-controlling personality, and the mutual communion of such personalities. For this reason duties to oneself, duties to one's neighbour, and duties to the community as a whole must also be characterised as purely formal. But the question still remains—what are the substantial ends which must be affirmed in order that such unity of personality and spiritualisation of a community can be developed? What are the concrete and substantial creations which the virtues of purity of character, of justice, and of solidarity must serve? Obviously these virtues all exist not for themselves alone, but as premises and means for uniting personalities in the pursuit of ends, which bestow upon them that substance in virtue of which they transcend nature. Morality is an indispensable premise for the realisation of substantial spiritual values, but it is not in itself an ultimate value, which bases itself solely upon its own worth. It can only work upon a substance which is not itself of a natural order, but is an overcoming both of the merely natural and actual life of instinct and of the struggle for existence. Thus the morality of personality, in consequence of its formality, demands an ideal concrete substance, in the realisation of which alone it is capable of attaining action and effect. On the other hand, the essential conception of ethical goods or cultural values requires an intention and power of action which is directed towards uniting the whole personality into something that exalts it above the ordinary life of instinct. The former cannot come into action without the latter; the latter can never become a reality without the former.

There is thus a close internal connection, as of two things which reciprocally condition one another. But however close the connection, it is yet obvious that the two spheres only meet to diverge. The morality of conscience originates in the aim of achieving the dignity and unity of the personality, and is therefore purely formal. Because of this quality of pure formality it is outside time or history.

Only in the manner and place of its appearance, and in the direction and definition of its application, is it historically conditioned. In itself, and in its own nature, it can be developed into a timelessly valid and comprehensive system of precepts. But it is quite otherwise with the ethical cultural values. They are entirely historical creations; they divide themselves into the various great cultural realms of the Family, the State, Law, the economic control of Nature, Science, Art, and Religion. Each of these different great realms has its own historical development, and each of its great historical manifestations is an individual creation, corresponding to the definite conditions of the period in which the general tendency of a given realm assumes a special form suitable only to the particular historical moment and the general situation.

It follows accordingly that these realms are decidedly not matters of Ethics, but rather belong to specific and independent sciences, which are termed "the systematic Mental Sciences." The Family is mainly the subject of the sciences of the sexual life and its sociological forms of organisation. The State, Law, and Society are subjects of political, legal, and social science; and technique and economics are subjects of the economic and technological sciences. Science itself furnishes a subject for Logic and for the history of Science and Philosophy; Art is a subject of Æsthetics; Religion a subject of Theology and the Philosophy of Religion. All these sciences deal with a vast field of historical material; they all seek the universal tendency which underlies the development of their spheres of life, the comprehension of the individual historical forms in which these spheres manifest their great contributions, and, in the last place, but only and entirely in the last place, the character which they should assume, in the present and in the future, in virtue of these developments and of our insight. It is only when these last endeavours are made that the sciences merge into Ethics. Considered in themselves, as sciences of pure understanding and historical investigation, they have no concern with Ethics.

When once they merge into Ethics, however, the question arises, how far these spheres of life have a common origin and a common aim, by virtue of which they may possibly be viewed in their totality as a manifestation of Mind over the various fields of its activity, in a definite form, on a large scale, and of a relatively permanent duration. Before their merger with Ethics this question could only be raised incidentally, and if it were desired to see and understand particular developments against the background of more general collective tendencies. But these were merely incidental aspects, and the attention speedily transferred itself from them to the special problem and the specific laws of the particular sphere of life as it stood. Some daring thinkers, standing on the borders of science, who love to derive all the expressions of the life of a whole period of history from a single spiritual basis, and to comprehend Antiquity, the Middle Ages, the Renaissance, and the like, as products of a collective mind, have stolen, as it were, for historical inquiry a problem which properly belongs to the final arbitrament of Ethics. But they have only treated it in a contemplative and expository sense, and the final ethical arbitrament must exhibit an active and formative character.

And here the main distinction between the morality of conscience and the ethic of cultural values becomes perfectly clear. As the former by virtue of its formality leads us out of History into the sphere of the timelessly valid, so conversely the latter conducts us back into History and Development, and more particularly into the realm of the Individual. Individuality bears an immeasurably greater significance in the latter than in the former. The morality of conscience becomes individualised in its application, but this individualisation is simply a limitation and definition of direction in the face of conflicting alternatives for which the individual conscience is responsible. The ethic of cultural values, on the other hand, leads us into the realm of the historical Particular in the more radical sense of a moulding of universal tendencies into historical creations of culture — a moulding which is peculiar, unique, and *sui generis* ; and here the whole spirit of an epoch, which, at the least, strongly influences such creations and co-ordinates them in a certain unity, is of itself a full individual system of thought in harmony with the whole set of conditions of the epoch. Chinese, Indian, Mohammedan, Hellenic, Mediæval, and Modern cultural atmospheres are individual systems of thought, mysterious and original, which express themselves even in Science and Religion. Here there is nothing independent of time and universally valid except the stimulus and obligation to create a system of culture.

This distinction is closely associated with another. The relation of the moral superstructure to the natural basis is different in the two cases. In the first case the relation of moral determination to the natural life of instinct is that of complete and total antithesis. In antithesis to that which is accidental and mutable stand Necessity and Uniformity; in antithesis to the eudæmonistic feeling of pleasure stands the feeling of obligation; in antithesis to the subjective impression stands an objective and universal actuality. This antithesis need not always result in strife and painful self-conquest, as the Stoics and Kant assert. It is also possible for the moral purpose to be accomplished easily, painlessly, and cheerfully, but even in this case its aim will be in antithesis to any process of tossing on the sea of passions, desires, and mere moods.

It is otherwise, however, with the antithesis between cultural values and the natural substratum of the instincts and their sociological implications from which those values emerge. Here a gradual detachment takes place in a sequence which moves step by step and never absolutely destroys the original relation. The ethical ideal of an alliance, at once personal and sexual, which in addition shall fulfil the functions of educating and ennobling future generations, detaches itself slowly, and by an infinite variety of methods, from the manifold organisations of the sexual life, which are intended to serve, as their first object, nothing but property, economics, or the needs of war. The technical-economic supremacy over Nature, which is also the presupposition for all higher spiritual existence, is slowly and laboriously wrung out of want, out of labour, out of the manufacture of tools, out of robbery and barter. The appreciation of Law and Justice, and of the value of State organisation, as means for the attainment of Freedom and Dignity, postulates ages of compulsion exercised by cruel, bellicose, and violent associations. Science originates in curiosity and the necessity for orientation ; Art in the play of imagination and the need for ornaments ; Religion in fear, anxiety, and the impression of permanent or temporary superhuman powers.

It is true that what detaches itself in the course of this development is something new—something no longer concerned with mere Desire, Pleasure, Need, or Compulsion. A higher and nobler essence emerges, and acquires an inherent value and devotion, even to the complete negation of the natural life of instinct. It is the source of all nobility and greatness in mankind, the foundation upon which the moral virtues and duties rest, the genuine inner essence of personality, which supplies a counterweight at once to the self-righteousness of moral advancement, and to the vain insurgence of a mere glorification of the natural and accidental Self. But the transition remains a gradual process. There never appears a sharply defined or radical antithesis, and in the issue there accordingly remains a permanent dependence on the natural basis and the temporary and special historic position of that basis. We may even say that the individuality of the cultural systems which arise in this way simply consists in the fact that the ideal essence enters in each case into an indissoluble union with the special natural condition and its complexities, by virtue of which such an ideal is at once conditioned by nature and ideal, at once lost and gained.

This is why these cultural values have so much closer a relation with history, in all its flux and vicissitudes, its combinations and its complexes, than has the morality of conscience. It is also the reason why the ethic of culture has a more vigorous and victorious influence than the morality of conscience. It is more necessary to the natural life of instinct, and at the same time less able to detach itself from that life, than is the morality of conscience. It is for this reason that cultural values, with their inherent appeal to the heart and their ennobling influence, can still endure when the moral forces are already shaken to their foundations. But it is also true that they cannot absolutely dispense with these forces; and at the last with the demoralisation of conscience there always ensues the downfall of culture also.

In these circumstances one may naturally expect that our main historico-philosophical problem—that of damming and controlling the historical stream—should present an easier solution within the domain of this sphere of Ethics than within that of the morality of conscience. That is indeed true, but not exactly in the way imagined by those who love simple ideals valid for all ages, irrespective of time and place, or hanker after Utopian ideals to be realised only in a distant future. Such thinkers, accordingly, ever since the time of Plato, have always preferred to sketch Utopian schemes or to spend their enthusiasm on the Progress which will necessarily realise their ideal; while practical reformers and men of action have had to be content with much more modest, more complicated, and more limited results.

If we now here look again for a clue in the history of Ethics to the manner in which the problem may be solved, we encounter a number of attempts to construct a system of values proceeding from a simple and single beginning to a simple and single goal. To such constructions it is natural to apply the demand that they should wear a practical and unitary shape. But it is no wonder that the methods of construction are much more difficult here than they were in the case of the morality of conscience, which, in view of its formality, can easily derive the particular rules from the basic form of reason which makes it a free postulating of unity and necessity.

This method is, however, much more difficult when we are dealing with the ethic of Culture, closely connected as it is with the various departments of practical life. For that purpose we are bound to assume a totally different conception of reason, as already charged with a concrete content. But in the opinion of many such a conception seems to be no longer a proper rational conception; and accordingly many thinkers, in dealing with this matter, prefer to speak of the great divinity " Nature " rather than of Reason, although they mean fundamentally the same. Plato, who in his *Republic* was the first to make the attempt, and thus to enter the realm of Utopian thought, did not even attempt a deduction, but felt, in typical Greek fashion, that the self-evident unity of body and mind, of mind and ideas, of divine essence and earthly existence, whether in the individual man or in the group or *Polis*, was a sacred thing, towards which Love ever strives under the influence of a natural compulsion. For the rest, he left it to dialectic and to the wisdom of the Rulers to abstract the several principles from their practical applications, and to combine them with the unity of the Good and the Beautiful.

The Neoplatonists and Christian philosophers afterwards, it is true, deduced a scale of values from the processes of Emanation and Remanation; but, in so doing, they directed their attention mainly to the distinction between the values of religion and those of mundane practice—the different values into which culture was in their opinion divided by a profound internal division. Plotinus still favoured a Utopian *Polis* or *Civitas Solis*, where both groups of values must be regarded as somehow combined in a unity. The members of the Christian Church found in the Church and its authority an agency which, for practical purposes, amalgamated the different values and decided their combination; while theory was content with vague generalities about an ascent from Nature to the Supernature of Grace which was at once a reversion and a conversion. Particular details—and this is already true as early as the time of St. Augustine—have to be collected from various utterances or read between the lines. Nor are we much better served by St. Thomas; and yet in the interval the casuistry of the confessional and the Christian *jus naturae* of the lawyers had in their different ways undertaken the codification, classification, and correlation of Values.

It was only in the great systems of the nineteenth century that new and original attempts were made to solve this problem, and only then was it thoroughly made the centre and pivot of Ethics. German speculative philosophy now attempted, through Schleiermacher and Hegel, a deduction from a new pantheistic concept. Schleiermacher deduced the cultural values from the state of tension between Reason and its object Nature; and he regarded this tension as expressing itself in the difference, first between a more individual and a more social, and then between a more contemplative and a more active attitude of Reason towards Nature. Thus he arrived at the values of the State, of Law, of Social Intercourse, of the Family, of Science, of Art and Religion. They remain essentially co-ordinated, and their temporary synthesis is a matter of special construction either by individual men or by phases of culture. Hegel, on the other hand, deduced from the innate ever-progressive dialectic of a Reason ever realising itself in Matter, first of all the subjective ethic of Conscience, then the objective ethic of State and Law, of Art and Religion, and finally the absolute ethic of Knowledge. This is a systematic genetic synthesis, rigorously directed towards a state of ideal perfection. Finally, the philosophers of the empiric and positivist schools of Western Europe deduced the values or goods from the development and transformation of individual men into members of a community, and the whole theme became a branch of Sociology, which represented to these thinkers both a philosophy of history and ethics.

The most perfect attempt in this direction was made by Herbert Spencer in the vast torso of his Sociology. There the place of a system of conceptual values is taken by the ideal of a balance between integration and differentiation of the body politic, resulting in the greatest possible happiness of the greatest possible number. Happiness is defined as man's technical, hygienic, and organising sovereignty over Nature, and the liberty and independence of mind which result from such supremacy. Science, art, and religion are regarded as historically conditioned means towards this end, because they help to create and keep together the body politic. Whittled down in such a manner, nothing remains of the three but an extended intellectualism which in the process has become entirely desiccated.

All these attempts at a deduction of the system of values, be they based on the nature of Reason, or on that of the Community, or on the World-process, or on the religious goal, are helpless in the face of the fullness and vigour, and also of the tensions and cross-purposes, of cultural values in real life. They only betray the conviction, which is no doubt justified, that those cultural values must have a common root, and that they always form a correlated connection in which the constituent members mutually affect one another. But we cannot by means of these attempts arrive at the common source from which these values arise, or at the law of their connection, or again at the law of change for the particular forms of the connection or for the temporary forms of the constituent members. We simply cannot formulate the world-process, because the cultural systems show such an enormous complexity in their interconnection and in their particular individual characteristics; and because, again, no goal common to all Mankind can be indicated. After Hegel's and Comte's failures in that direction, we are entitled to assume this, at any rate, as the irrefutable result of all the discussions about the logic and philosophy of history.

A task that cannot be avoided, however, is the welding together of these cultural values into a homogeneous whole for the Present and the Future within a large given area of Culture. Here, and here alone, is the one possibility of a solution for our problem—the problem of damming and controlling the historical stream of life.

But how can it be attained? In the first place it cannot be attained at all through conscious work and theoretical construction. It takes place within the sphere of the unconscious. The evolution of the individual constituent parts themselves, as well as that of their mutual relations, develops under the pressure of factors quite unnoticed by those who suffer it—the pressure of geographical and climatic influences, of the scope available for migration and nutrition, of the number of births and the biological constitution generally; and finally there is the influence of individual mental peculiarities, which are usually labelled as fundamental racial or national characteristics, because one has no further or other explanation for them. To this must be added the influence of special historical events, of the social structure usually connected with them, and of the leading personalities, who are incalculable gifts of Fate, and whose influence transforms itself into a tradition by which multitudes are swayed. Under all these conditions, and under the stimulus of reason, as it raises itself above Nature and proceeds to organise Nature, there is evolved, without our being aware or taking note of it, a system of Values as a pure fact, neither produced by thought nor directed by volition. It becomes a system from time to time partly through the power (for whatever reason it may be triumphant) of a single central value, which unites with itself in a more or less clear and energetic manner all the other values, and partly in virtue of the logic and the development of the consequences immanent in such tendencies. These consequences, too, develop at first unnoticed, and are only lifted from time to time into the light of consciousness by leading personalities. Thus in China there predominates the idea of the large family, in the upper classes of India the idea of contemplative religion ; the Greek genius was swayed by Art, the Roman by the ideas of State and Law ; the Christian sphere of culture was one of an amalgamation, full of tensions, between the values of our earthly world and those of the supramundane world of religion. Whether such a system can develop at all depends on the breadth and depth of the original endowment and on the favour of historical destiny. Sometimes it may never get beyond a tangle of confused interplay ; and in moments of crisis such a tangle may be found even in the great systems of culture, though these systems, it is true, coalesce anew in periods of Renascence and Reformation.

These syntheses, produced unconsciously, but fundamental and fateful in their nature, are primarily decisive. But in all moments of crisis, and in periods of greater maturity, a conscious and constructive synthesis also becomes necessary. This kind of synthesis is the something for which to-day we are searching unceasingly in our modern world.

The final question, therefore, is, " how can that synthesis be achieved ? "

Here, it is true, we are dealing with a

matter of theoretical construction. But this construction is not an *a priori* construction which can start from the essential nature of Reason or the law of the world-process. It is rather an *a posteriori* construction which essentially demands a knowledge of the premises, history, and destiny of the particular sphere of culture. Such a synthesis must try to discover and mentally assimilate the premises and bases of its own existence, as they have been shaped in unconscious processes— the geographical and biological conditions of its own sphere of life; the logical necessity of the development which it has undergone; the interplay of Necessity and Chance. Definite possibilities and methods are thus indicated from the very first and for every synthesis; and in following these we are only concerned with the historical individuality of the particular sphere of Culture, and the peculiarity of Reason as it has developed here in this given place.

Once, however, this knowledge has been attained, the system thus evolved must be refined, concentrated, liberated, and directed. The essential point is to determine the direction by bringing out the central value and attaching and incorporating with it the rest. The value of what we thus choose as the

THE ETHICS OF CULTURAL VALUES

central value and thus make the pivot of organisation can only be based on a personal impression of the claims of reality and of our own conscience. The manner and method in which the other values are connected with the central value thus attained is similarly, in the last resort, an act in a personal life, which can only afterwards be expressed as a system and justify itself by its results. The creative act, and a conscience ready to assume responsibility, are here too the decisive factors, no less than in the application of the morality of conscience to the complicated relations of reality.

It is, too, the personal and individual conscience which connects the system of cultural values with that of the morality of conscience —explaining and strengthening, and at the same time conditioning and limiting, the one by the other. For the establishment of this connection there is no *a priori* system available; the only means is the tact and energy of the acting and shaping mind, which only at a later date precipitates the unity of its life in the unity of thought presented in such a system of the two Ethics. Fundamentally such a system can only present itself as a living deed and an historical achievement, resting upon an understanding of the whole evolutionary process leading towards us and upon the courage to refashion and further develop it. Statesmen, reformers, poets, prophets, are usually active agents in this work. In spite of all their most elaborate reflections they can at bottom adduce for themselves no other plea than that of Jesus: " He who is of the truth heareth My voice." That the claimant himself is " of the truth " is a thing which he can only believe and finally prove by throwing his life into the scale. Only doctrinaires turn such certainty into *a priori* systems proceeding on exact logical lines; and the empiricists, seeing everywhere but details, turn it into commonplace platitudes and then into scepticism.

Here, too, it is faith that ultimately decides; and here, too, it is likewise faith that justifies. It is not by any peradventure that the religious idea of our Western sphere of culture culminates in this doctrine; and this doctrine of justification by faith is valid equally for Catholics and for Protestants. They differ with regard to the Authority to be acknowledged and the meaning to be attached to the content of the Religious Value. But for both the proof of Authority is Faith—an inward personal experience and a personal attitude; and in both this Faith proves itself by its fruits.

The same was also true of Plato's Idea of the Good ; of the teleological system and entelechy of Aristotle ; of the *jus naturae* of the Stoics. In lay theories of culture also this was finally the essence ; but lay thinkers for the most part failed to see the element of faith in their theories as clearly as the theologians. And in the last resort they are not so far asunder from one another in the contents they thus affirm as they are fain to imagine. The idea of Personality, which, in the form of Freedom, determines everything in the morality of conscience, and, in the form of Object, everything in the ethic of values—this idea is, after all, a Western belief, unknown, in our sense, to the Far East, and pre-eminently and peculiarly the destiny of us Europeans. But in view of the whole of our history we cannot but believe that it is for us the truth.

3
DER GEMEINGEIST

3

THE COMMON SPIRIT

Translated by Professor H. G. Atkins, *of King's College, London.*

Carefully revised by Principal Barker *and* Baron Hügel.

3

THE COMMON SPIRIT

THE argument of the first two lectures has led us to conclude that the stream of historical life may be dammed and controlled from two separate sides. On the one hand we have the morality of conscience, which for us Europeans has its principal foundations in the Stoic-Christian ideas, and leads, in one form or another, to the ideas of the Rights of Man, Humanity, and the Duties of Solidarity. This realm of thought received its expression for centuries in Christian and profane Natural Law, and was only translated by Kant from the language of the concept of Nature into that of the concept of moral obligation. This Kantian modification is of great formal importance, and heightens the forces at work in the contrast between the world which the conscience has to construct, and the mere stream of the world of historical facts and developments, which is always fusing into one another the natural and the ethical, the sensuous and the spiritual. On the other hand this damming and controlling can also be achieved by the Ethic of the Cultural Values, which for us Europeans was most decisively formulated by Plato and Neo-Platonism.

The Christian period closely associated this ethic with the morality of Conscience, thus throwing into prominent relief the categorical character of the moral goods or values, and effecting a centralisation around the religious value, now no longer regarded as merging into the others. The modern spirit secularised this Platonic-Christian tradition, and produced a notable development in the philosophy of German Idealism, which springs principally from Neoplatonic-Christian roots, but has added to Platonism the idea of Individuality, that child of the Middle Ages, Mysticism, and the Renaissance. The thought of Western Europe, on the other hand, where it no longer follows Platonism and the Christian doctrine of Authority, usually derives the doctrine of the ethical Goods or Values, no less than the morality of Conscience, from the concept of Nature. The result is generally a system of utilitarianism, based in one form or another on sociological foundations and inspired by sociological aims, which is marked by a lofty idealism and yet imbued with the notion of progress according to natural law. In point of content, however, the object sought is everywhere (alike in Germany and in Western Europe) the same: it is a union of the Morality of Conscience with the Ethic of the Goods or Values. In this union the former is everywhere essentially uniform; the latter varies greatly with various races and epochs. Nevertheless the two principles, which must constantly be associated afresh, can really solve in co-operation our present problem.

This solution of the problem, however, is always an association of different principles, and an application, too, of these associated principles to the facts and needs of the natural, sensuous process, with its innumerable accidents and actualities, which are not determined by the Idea, and can never be completely dominated by it. This accounts for the character of struggle and labour that is inseparably associated with this solution, and indeed with Ethics in general; it explains its irrevocable diversity and its qualities of compromise and individuality, which always emerge afresh and refuse to yield to mere brute fact. In this compromise there is, properly understood, something more than a simple coming to terms with the complications of life. There is a deeper content; there is the metaphysical character of individuality which attaches to all personal decisions of conscience and to every synthesis of cultural values. Finally, it is in this character of individuality that the imperfectibility of all ethical sciences has also its roots; for Ethics, whilst it can lay foundations in a sense that is universally valid, can never determine its results in a sense that is also equally valid for all time. Herein resides its essential and inevitable imperfectibility, both as a science and in actual life, which predestines it to be the most incomplete of all the philosophical sciences. On the other hand, there is in particular syntheses, when they are made with a wide vision and deep thought, something objective and of a universal validity, which is ever pressing forward, and, in its special individual application to place and condition, can rather be felt than intellectually constructed. And this feeling, joined to broad and objective considerations, establishes sufficient security against all scepticism and all fundamental relativism. Scepticism and relativism are only an apparently necessary consequence of modern intellectual conditions and of Historicism. They can be overcome by way of Ethics, and by way of the ideal forces emerging from history itself, which are only mirrored and concentrated in Ethics.

But it cannot be denied that this objectivity is involved in a deep subjectivity and founded on personal resolve. One cannot doubt the existence of such objectivity for the person engaged in action or decision ; but it remains a highly individual and personal matter. But if that be so, this solution appears to be inadequate for that purpose of damming and controlling the stream of life which we have in view. The real solution demands mass-convictions, common spirit, broad driving-power, public opinion. And so there arises finally the question of the relation of our solution to this need of a broad common spirit moulding the masses and the successive generations. How can such a personal and individual solution develop into a common spirit, which, after all, presupposes something super-individual and universal? The very curse and torment of the modern world seems to be that it only knows the directive forces of the mind as particular realities at play by the side of one another. In the form of Liberalism and Tolerance, and under the guise of mutual complement and mutual enrichment, this mode of thought appeared at first to be a release from the shackles of religious confessions, the State, and education. In its final development it appears to be the tragic or comic end of Liberalism, and to lead to dissolution, decomposition, and spiritual anarchy, which are all opposed in their turn by renaissances of ecclesiastical or rationalistic dogmas.

Here we have without doubt one of the most difficult and painful problems of the present day. Our solution cannot be accepted—at any rate it cannot be essentially accepted—in the form of this Liberalism, which is all too credulous of harmony and all too egocentric. Our conception of individuality must be different from that of average Liberalism. But by us too the solution itself must undoubtedly be sought in the direction of the conception of individuality.

It is surely abundantly evident that, in those yearning glorifications of the public spirit in which we fail, there is to be found much sentimental phantasy and weakness of will, much romantic idealisation of the past and the future. We dream into the past a religious, ethical, and artistic public spirit, which we believe we apprehend in its dogmas and manners, in its monuments and literatures, and which, if we allow for the remoteness of the times, in comparison with the present actually exists. Thus the Middle Ages and pre-democratic Greece have been especially glorified and still are glorified to-day. This is the ground of catholicising or classicising flights from the actual or imagined anarchy of the present; it is the source of our dreams and demands for a future marked by a pacified unity and solidarity in the feelings and practical institutions of life, a future in which Individualism and its supposed correlative, Intellectualism, will be surmounted, and everything will be permeated by a vital rhythm at once calmer and more assured. Our own times appear to us again and again plunged in a state of anarchy and interminable conflict of individual idiosyncrasies. This has even been raised to the dignity of a law of sociological development. Starting from Sir Henry Maine's distinction of Status and Contract, Ferdinand Tönnies, the distinguished investigator of the development of sociological ideas from Hobbes to Herbert Spencer, has constructed a series of cultural epochs, which begins with the Community, as a substance by which the individuals are mystically supported, proceeds to Society, as a purposive and rational contractual relationship of sovereign individuals, and then struggles through violent revolutions towards the goal of Socialism. St. Simon and Comte have propounded a similar doctrine with the help of different concepts. Goethe's transition to Classicism and the cult of Hellenism, and in the other direction the leanings of the Romanticists towards the Middle Ages, must be similarly interpreted, even though they have less modern aims. From this point of view the present day is assumed to be the epoch of intellectualistic Individualism, of eclectic Historicism, of co-ordinating Liberalism, of languid philosophic Tolerance. The deduction is then made that it is fundamentally impossible to solve our present problem on the basis of modern society. Indeed one might be tempted to regard the solution I have given as the typical expression of these highly individualistic, liberal, and anarchical basic conditions, if such a solution were more common than it actually is. Literally, at any rate, it seems to apply exactly to individualistic society. Wilhelm von Humboldt's early work, published long after his death, on the "Limits of the State" (*Grenzen des Staates*), a work admired by John Stuart Mill, seems already to have adumbrated such a form of Liberalism. The present anarchy of values and of mind appears to be only the natural consequence, and the curve of this school of thought seems already to have passed its zenith.

That, however, is not the meaning of the ethico-metaphysical conception of Individuality, as it is presented here in the combination of the Morality of Conscience and that of the Ethic of the Cultural Values with the conception of a Creative Compromise adapted to each successive stage of development. This conception has nothing to do with supine liberalism and promiscuous tolerance. It demands an attitude to the trend of development, as intuitive and constructive thought is certain to be bound to see it from its own standpoint; it demands the staking of our whole courage for that which each personally and individually holds to be certain. Here the solution means no feeble tolerance, but rather struggle and endurance. The proof of the correctness of one's own position consists in an individual adjustment of the kind described, and in the certainty which results therefrom; and in this respect this solution is no doubt appropriate to a cultural epoch possessing neither the dogmatic force of universally prevalent ecclesiastical dogmas, nor the illusion of a rationalistic, natural, intellectual proof; an age, moreover, arrived at that state of mature differentiation which has raised a strong intellectual section of the community above the level of average material interests and social conventions. For various reasons, it is true, this applies to the various peoples of our cultural sphere in varying degrees, and as a result the urgent need for the solution proposed also varies in different countries. But the predominance of an intellectual class is nevertheless everywhere a result of culture, and it therefore denotes, in some degree or other, the emancipation of ideas from mere tradition and authority. If I confine myself to those German conditions with which I am most familiar, I find a very broad and very strongly differentiated intellectual class, coupled with a great diversity of material conditions of existence which are nowhere clearly and simply defined, and with a social convention which varies greatly in the various classes.

Thus, even for external reasons alone, there is a great lack of homogeneity. And when we regard the position internally this lack is not less pronounced. Within the intellectual class the traditions of the Enlightenment of Western Europe are in conflict with those of German romantic-classical Idealism, while the latter, the real main force of German thought, is again fundamentally dissolved by those terrible epigoni of German idealism, Karl Marx and Friedrich Nietzsche, who are in their universal idealism its perpetuators and in their atheism the destroyers of its traditions from two diametrically opposite sides. In these circumstances an individual position is quite unavoidable, but it cannot be regarded as a harmless variation within a homogeneous whole. No mere play of various individualities, with a final levelling of all in one common mean, is possible ; it requires a conflict, which reminds us of the conflicts of the ages of the religious confessions and their religious wars, and which will also call the old confessional forces of the churches into the field. But the proofs which have to be adduced for the positions here to be vindicated can be no other than those already described, and so far as the resultant public spirit depends on the nature of the proofs, it will, like them, be strongly particularised, and will show their nature and character. But what thus applies to Germany applies also *mutatis mutandis* to the other cultural lands, and for them too the solution cannot be essentially different.

Before, however, we go further into this question, a few words must be said of the whole conception of a common spirit, and also of the modifications which it undergoes in the typical sequence of cultural epochs. In the present connection it is a matter of comparative indifference how one defines and explains it conceptually ; whether, like the German Romantic theory, one conceives of it somewhat mystically as a common spiritual substance pervading the individual, or, like the sociologists of Western Europe, as a resultant of typical fundamental impulses, the intellectual and the emotional ; whether with Schleiermacher we trace it to an oscillation of the reason between the impulse towards identity and that towards differentiation, or with Gabriel Tarde to inter-individual adaptations and imitations, and therefore, in the last resort, to the realisation of individual initiatives ; or whether finally we explain it, with the aid of the analogies from vitalistic biology which are so popular in the mental sciences to-day, by a kind of organic vital unity and correlation of the group. Explain it how we may, the fact itself is beyond doubt, as is its decisive importance for the solution of our problem. Moreover, the variety of the sociological structures of the successive typical cultural epochs must not be exaggerated and over-estimated. It is true that the

Middle Ages and the individualised epochs of maturity show in this respect a different structure, to say nothing of the structure of primitive times, on which little light has yet been thrown. In the Middle Ages, with their scanty population, restricted intercourse, and undeveloped intellectual life, we find communities whose forms are determined by nature and blood, by the system of payment in kind and by military associations, all of which finds its expression in the existence of special types of law, religion, and custom. In the epochs of maturity population, intercourse, and technical skill increase, and groups are much more firmly based on conscious and purposive agreement ; the individual becomes free ; thought and feeling find the need and the possibility of an almost infinitely differentiated expression. All the same the Middle Ages are not so instinctive and spontaneous as Romanticism would have us believe, and their spiritual unity seen at close range is full of conflict and friction. Men fight for nuances as fiercely as they do to-day for principles, and the passion for differentiation, where its operation is not yet possible in the intellectual sphere, finds a channel in the material and personal sphere in the shape of endless feuds. On the other hand the epochs of maturity are rich in common moods, hypotheses, and conventions; filled with vague mass-impulses and tyrannical dogmas; little guided, on the whole, by rational purpose, but driven by passions and feelings. Conversely, a great levelling takes place through law, intercourse, and education; and these epochs display the greatest skill in the creation of public spirit. The conventions of modern culture, seen from a distance, are perhaps not much more anarchical than was mediæval Catholicism with all its endless conflicts. The great difference is that the sections of the population involved in the struggles and nuances are to-day broader and more conscious, and in this respect, too, the difference between the various cultured nations is very considerable. A paradise of public opinion like America has perhaps not much less public spirit than the more vegetative periods of the Middle Ages.[1]

However, the question that we have further to discuss is not connected with these points.

[1] I take this to mean that in the United States of to-day, modern as its society may be, public opinion is so strong, and controls the individual so much, that we may say that there is almost as much " public spirit " dominating its thought as there was even in those periods of the Middle Ages which were least troubled by the strain of controversy and individual views.—E. B.

Explain it as we will, Common Spirit remains Common Spirit, and without this super-individualism no strong and healthy ethical direction of the stream of life is at all possible. However far the distinction between the predominance of instinct and that of conscious, scientific, systematic thought may differentiate the cultural epochs, we must admit that even in the epochs of cultural maturity the Common Spirit exists as a fact and a necessity, and that if it becomes too far decomposed it has to undergo a re-creation which does not depend on the predominance of instinct and natural conditions, but can also be achieved by process of thought. The decisive point is the realisation that monistic conceptions of Common Spirit are a fantastic delusion. No Present has ever had such a view of itself; it has existed only in those Utopian longings to create an ideal future or revive a golden past which produced the ideals of the Golden Age and Paradise, no less than the expectations of the Platonic Republic and the Christian Kingdom of God. The truth is that there has never been any Common Spirit but that of a group, family, race, class, profession, school, or sect, and even the Church's attempt to comprehend all these, as it were, under a single dome remained, in the time of its real and complete domination, a work of force and diplomacy, a faith and a dream, contradicted in the actual life of the times by the eternal strife of ideas and interests.

For the Present especially with which alone we are here immediately concerned, this is plainly evident. It has perhaps a universal Common Spirit, which can only be seen in complete detachment, by strangers and those who will come after us, but aids us little, because we take it for granted and as self-evident, in achieving our present purpose. But it is rather the case that our lives are passed from the first not in a monistic, homogeneous circle, but in a number of circles, each of which has its own ethical Common Spirit. The facts of life show, within the atmosphere which surrounds us and is therefore incomprehensible to us, a multiplicity of Common Spirits or Social Complexes, which have each their own intellectual foundation. Enumerating roughly and proceeding from the general to the particular, we may tabulate them as follows:

1. Humanity;
2. The sphere of Western culture;
3. The Nation;
4. The social class;

5. The Family;
6. The free professional associations;
7. The narrower circles based on sympathy or friendship;
8. The communities of creed, church, and denomination;
9. The free intellectual communities or schools of thought.

Each has a different intellectual content. It is absolutely impossible to conceive of them all as one community, and then to credit this community ideally with a common intellectual content. The claims of the churches in this direction are not realisable; but they are also only apparent. In truth the ethical normative ideas of the churches, so far as they transcend the purely personal and the narrower circles of private life, are themselves a helpless conglomerate. And the same is the case with the philosophical ethical systems. They cannot conceive and cannot realise the unitary community and the unitary spirit. In the ethical systems either the most various elements are mingled, with the result that they diverge widely in practice, or their conception is purely formal, and they satisfy only the unitary requirements of a logical asceticism. Even socialism, which aims at overcoming what it regards as purely bourgeois anarchy by a tyrannically circumscribed picture of history and civilisation, remits every serious consideration to an unknown future or confines itself merely to economic and class ethics.

All of this is not a curse and special fate of the present day, though its growth of population, its social and intellectual differentiation, and its break with tradition and authority have intensified and deepened the plurality. It is especially true that the present sees everything in a wider horizon, in more complicated relations, and with a more conscious deliberation of aims. At the same time authority and tradition have survived in many forms, or have been constructed anew; imitation, the herd instinct, poverty of thought, and a consequent susceptibility to influence remain; and in addition the intellectual contents of interests, both broad and narrow, and of blood-groups still bulk large. Moved by their generally obvious material interests, and in moments of real or imaginary danger, the groups merge into Common Spirit, even as they did in the most primitive ages. Yet in the religious and metaphysical sphere we may certainly trace a rapidly increasing anarchy, and this is what has to be faced. For that purpose, however, other means will be necessary.

These means must not be sought in the sphere of monistic conceptions of an all-embracing Common Spirit and in corresponding measures of a policy of national or ecclesiastical education. Generally speaking, it is a fact that we live in various social complexes which are in the last resort concentric and each of which has its own intellectual content. This content is determined by the nature of the complexes concerned, and it is in general not nearly so problematical as the tortured modern soul conceives it to be. One has only to resolve to let each complex go untroubled on its way, and to live in each according to its own special demands, without elevating any one of them monistically into a universal basis or a single all-determining accent. One can only demand for the most universal community, which is that of *Humanity*, a mutual understanding and tolerance, and a feeling of fundamental human obligation, without any very definite content. In doing so we may, with complete propriety, make essential distinctions according to the stage of cultural development of the different races and groups. For one's own *Cultural Sphere* there can only be an understanding of its historical import, and within it a feeling of the solidarity of the closer relationships. For the rest, the distinctions will remain clearly perceptible, and the bridges will always communicate rather between individual and individual than between race and race. It is the task of the great poets and historians to educate and to represent this public feeling, and of this European literature has long had magnificent examples to show. For the *National Community* the love of home, native soil, and mother tongue, a common sense of honour and freedom and independence, with all the necessary virtues of bravery and wisdom, will suffice. For the rest the differences of race, profession, and class will be insurmountable, and the religious and philosophical element will remain free from national constraint and monism, however little this may be in the spirit of modern nationalism. This latter is one of the most dangerous monistic exaggerations of the idea of a Common Spirit, and is a special hindrance to the solution of our present problem. For the *Family*, finally, which with us has sunk from the family in the wider to that in the narrower sense, and has thereby lost in general significance for mental development, the physiologically determined feelings of love and of the linking of the generations, the socially determined feelings of family honour and filial duty, the duties of mutual aid and of common obligation, will suffice. Everything else within it remains free, and is naturally capable of great individual differentiation. Of the special associations and social circles there is no need to speak further, as the essentials are self-evident.

In all these complexes we live simultaneously, without difficulty and without confusion. If we seek to give them an association and a connection, to conceive of them not as co-ordinated but as concentric circles, we find ourselves at once confronted with the metaphysical and religious element, which alone can unite them under one common dome. This the Churches did formerly, but they can no longer do it to-day, even in the manner of compromise adopted in former days. Apart from all other obvious reasons, it is impossible for the simple reason that they are themselves a Plural, and that there is here no longer any Singular. For this most fundamental question of Ethics all that is left to-day is the individual and personal combination of the morality of the Conscience, of the Cultural Values, and of the given situation, of which we have spoken above. With us, accordingly, any Public Spirit of a metaphysical-religious nature can only arise and operate alongside and outside the churches—and often enough, we must admit, also within them—in a way that is in keeping with such a basis.

And here we are confronted with the heart of the problem, and at the same time the only kind of solution adequate to the present day becomes clear. We see it already being followed by the practice of modern nations, especially by the fervent demands of modern youth, Leagues of Youth, Christian, philosophical, humanistic associations, and unions of all kinds.

Wherever the modern conditions are understood, we see the demand for more originality and more community; in other words, the instinctive demand for the personal and creative disposition of the individual synthesis, combined with a deep feeling for its inner necessity. It is equally true that this synthesis is demanded, not as an interesting or tolerable play of personal mood and opinion, but as the outcome of a feeling of responsibility and the communicative impulse of an overflowing love. The spiritual forces must be created and moulded, not in self-centred solitude, or intellectually and in literature, but with an active and basic purpose of direction towards intimate community, leadership, and self-communication. A new salvation, to be found in fresh and original concentration on a metaphysical foundation; a new love, resting on the feeling of all spiritual values as fundamentally common values—this is the form in which the universal validity of these syntheses can emerge into a Common Spirit. "The new salvation can come only from new love," says one of the greatest German poets of the present day. Here we are thinking of no new universal religion and of no mere philanthropy, but of personal unions for intercourse and education, in which leading personalities will mould the fundamental ethical synthesis and establish its final religious and metaphysical convictions.

It is germ-cells of a new spiritual freshness, power, concentration, and discipline, which have everywhere to be formed against the crudity, shallowness, and vulgarity of a trivialised or caricatured, increasingly disintegrated and desolate civilisation. In the nature of things they must begin in a small way and assume an individual form in accordance with individual impulse. And this is actually the case at the present time. Wherever we look to-day, such germ-cells are forming; everywhere they are striving to spread abroad, especially in the form of personal communion and love, the universal and inevitable elements comprised in their particular synthesis. The nature of the further development along these lines is a question in itself which cannot yet be answered to-day. From these germ-cells there must proceed great fighting forces of public life. Since in the personal and particular they seek to find the Universal and Love, they will meet, embrace, and amalgamate. Thence may proceed that measure of public spirit in the final ethical foundations which alone is possible for modern peoples. With its help they will perhaps reanimate their torpid churches, and on this basis the final possibilities of our modern world, in the form of the types developing in it, will be elaborated. Even so there will be no monistic unitary society. There never was such a thing; and the unity of the modern mind which, at the best, is exceedingly relative, will be naturally much more diversified than that of the Middle Ages.

But a new field must be ploughed, and it is only in this way that the impulse towards a new ethical synthesis can attain its appropriate public spirit. Strong emphasis must therefore be laid on the fact that this central synthesis concerns those very religious and metaphysical foundations from which the real fusing warmth and glow of life proceeds.

The actual particular complexes mentioned above will continue to exist in relative independence, and what will be implanted in them is but the unifying root-force, which makes them ramifications of the fundamental spiritual position of man in the universe.

The task of the damming and controlling of the stream of historical life is thus on all sides complicated. It involves a combination of the various fundamental tendencies of the ethical consciousness, and the only evidence which can ever be deduced for the decisive combinations is but a conviction of faith based on conscience and conditioned by individuality. The solution thus gained, which we have to regard as a central solution achieved in a metaphysical-religious nucleus, can only be spread from individual centres, and made into a spirit of self-communication and love, which will as far as possible spread itself over the widest circles, but will always be at war with other forms of belief. Such central ethical forces, however, have by their side a wealth of more peripheral circles, which receive from their natural foundations a simpler and more assured ethical regulation, and thus make life relatively independent of such central decisions, though at the same time they constantly require to be reincorporated in them.

It is now clear what is meant when one describes all Ethics as something complex and diversified. With these complex forces it is possible to dam and control the stream of life. But every such control is always, by reason of this complexity, a struggle; it is ever changing; it develops ethical public spirit along various lines, and only exceptionally and in a narrower circle is it of centrally binding force. As no unified church any longer exercises this binding force, the task has devolved upon a number of churches, and also, and along with them, upon personal associations and leagues, which are a substitute for the churches, and will themselves have to strive to become a kind of church.

The task of damming and controlling is therefore essentially incapable of completion and essentially unending; and yet it is always soluble and practicable in each new case. A radical and absolute solution does not exist; there are only working, partial, synthetically uniting solutions. Yet the stream of life is always surging upward and onward. History within itself cannot be transcended, and knows of no salvation except in the form of devout anticipations of the Hereafter, or glorified transfigurations of partial salvations. The Kingdom of God and Nirvana lie outside all history. In history itself there are only relative victories; and these relative victories themselves vary greatly in power and depth, according to time and circumstance.

This may suffice for the practical purposes of human action, and indeed it only reflects the actual course of events. Whosoever is discontented with it must direct his gaze beyond the bounds of history. If there is any solution at all of these riddles and problems, with their conflicts and contradictions, that solution certainly is not to be found within their own sphere, but beyond it, in that unknown land, of which there are so many indications in the historic struggle of the spirit upwards, but which itself is never revealed to our eyes.

But even for those who fix their gaze on that unknown land, the actual course and struggle of life remain the same as before, and the ethical mastery of the stream of life becomes no stronger and no more complete. They are only able to affirm those indications more joyfully, and to feel them more fully, than those whose hopes are bounded by this life.

Section III

POLITIK, PATRIOTISMUS, RELIGION

A Lecture written for delivery before the London Society for the Study of Religion in March 1923.

Section III

POLITICS, PATRIOTISM, AND RELIGION

Translated by Miss Mary E. Clarke, *Graduate in Philosophy of the University of London.*

Carefully revised by Baron F. von Hügel *and* Mr. Edwyn Bevan.

III

POLITICS, PATRIOTISM, AND RELIGION

I SHOULD naturally like to begin by expressing to you my sincere thanks for the great honour you have done me in inviting me to address one of your meetings. I think I am in agreement with the general religious principles for which your Society stands, and the subject you have asked me to discuss seems to me to be in harmony with this general theoretical standpoint. Certainly it was easier to treat such a subject from the theoretical point of view ten years ago than it is to-day, when it has acquired such an exceedingly painful practical significance, and when it vibrates, as the keenest of its pains, within all the present suffering of mankind. I will try, however, to avoid these practical difficulties and to confine myself entirely to the general theoretical aspect of the subject. Even so, the difficulties which it presents will be sufficiently great.

The first object to which we must direct our attention are, of course, the forces of politics and ethical religion, as they stand over against each other in all the countries of the world. The term "politics" hardly requires much definition, I think. It is the art of organising a community into a permanent order within itself, and of maintaining and extending this community, so organised, in the world at large. The means employed to this end are partly psychological influence, partly the actual instruments of force—the army and the police. Every such organisation is thus dependent upon the geographical position of the original settlement, the rate of increase in its population, and the ambition and acquisitive instincts of such several groups of mankind. An unfavourable position or scattered settlement involves warfare with neighbouring tribes; a rising birth-rate leads to emigration and colonisation or to the extension of boundaries. From ambition arise the heroic passions: desire for fame, glory, and power; whilst the instinct of acquisition engenders the restless desire for a rising standard of living.

Now, all these characteristics and consequences of the consolidation of political power are easy enough to reconcile with the tribal and national religions of pagan races. The deities of these races are identified with the tribe or with its rulers. These rulers are descendants or incarnations of the gods, or at any rate stand in very close relation to them. War-gains and conquests are the works and gains of the gods themselves; so, too, are internal order, power, and tribal custom. A defeat is a defeat of the gods, and the worshippers transfer their allegiance to the deities proved stronger. Their moral code is more or less connected with their religious cult. It is primarily a morality of warriors and heroes, according to the character of the gods worshipped in such religions. If the claims of justice and of personal dignity are recognised at all, they appear here, at most, as part of an inter-tribal morality applying only to the members of the clan; they do not extend to other tribes, to barbarians, enemies, or unbelievers, to slaves or manual workers. The problem of the mutual relations of religion and politics does not arise at this stage. Political theory and religion are both still naturalistic. Both worship strength and power and the success which is procured by the natural capacities and the natural circumstances of mankind. Only the morality of heroic valour lends, to the ancient Indians and to the great figures of Homeric legend, a certain supernaturalistic greatness.

The situation, however, becomes quite different when we arrive at the universal, ethical religions. I call them "universal" because they acknowledge one unifying Power behind phenomena, and "ethical" because man's relation to the Power is here recognised as of necessity a personal and spiritual relation. Only from the point of view of the spirit and of morality can there be unity, not from the point of view of nature. True, this morality is a very different morality from that of the natural groups of families and clans. It is a morality whose centre of gravity lies in the worship of, and devotion to, the Divine, and which ultimately measures the worth of a man according to the degree of such devotion attained by him. The heroic virtues of the warrior thus drop into the background, if they do not disappear altogether or are proscribed. Clearly, however, the relation between ethical religion and politics becomes now a very difficult problem, for politics remain attached to this or that particular State, and seem to require, above all the other virtues, the heroic qualities of the warrior.

It is thus an historical fact that a religion of this type has seldom exercised a really determining influence upon political theory and practice—indeed, there are really only two examples of this, viz. China, when the Confucian ethic was at the zenith of its influence, and mediæval Europe. Buddhism, which perhaps presents the opposition to the spirit of politics in its most acute form, has, for this very reason, failed to attain any influence in the political sphere. It has remained merely one element in the national life of the countries into which it has penetrated; it has not become a ruling force among them.

Judaism has had a political creed, but only as a dream and a hope of the future, ever since it freed itself from the politics of the Davidic Kings; in a time of tribulation it has built up a visionary political ideal out of religious faith and religious morals. Its Messianic hopes still essentially retain the old political ideal of Jewish dominion; indeed they even extend this ideal to that of a world-dominion. Wherever these conceptions keep their hold, there the Jewish precepts of patience and long-suffering, of earnestness and compassion, constitute an " interim ethic " only.

Islam, a system closely related to Judaism, is frankly a religion of warriors of the nomadic Arabian tribes; and opposition to unbelievers at home and abroad is fundamental to it. So far as this religion has influenced politics at all, it has not been by way of opposition to them, for Islam is itself a political creed—a creed at the level when morality is still circumscribed by the community.

Lastly, in the religion of old Persia, which so profoundly influenced Judaism, we also see, in spite of its many ethical and spiritual features, a national religion, inspiring its peasant and warrior classes with strength for the fight to preserve their nationality and their culture.

It is true that in none of these cases have the basic principles been at any time very rigorously maintained; they have undergone modifications and humanisation in the flux and reflux of history. But these modifications have always been inconsistent with their fundamental positions, and have never enabled them to exercise any determining influence upon politics or bring them nearer to a really humanitarian standpoint. And so China and mediæval Europe remain the only two exceptions we have to consider.

The religion of China under Confucianism is a greatly diluted and very abstract religion. In the last resort it is little more than a belief in a universal world-order, in which the rules of morality have also their foundation. But these rules are genuinely moral; they are rules for the maintenance of peace under a patriarchal order of life and for the cultivation of the domestic virtues—sincerity, dignity, courtesy, the industrious pursuit of culture, and the development of a peaceful communal spirit. As a result, China has possessed, in many respects, the most prosperous and the healthiest social and political order in the world; but it was feeble in its external action, and it suffered the evils of over-population without knowing how to remedy them, unless plague or famine relieved its government of the task. But let us leave China aside. It may for a time have actually constituted a moral idyll and a pattern of social virtue, but it can give us no help in the solution of our present European problems.

Europe has inherited, both from the old classical civilisation and from mediæval barbarism, a bent towards the titanic which dares everything and effects everything, a spirit of adventure which goes forth to explore and to conquer the world. Its symbol is Prometheus stealing fire from the gods, accomplishing everything by his own strength, and the Viking discovering and conquering new worlds. It is here that the problem of " Politics and Religion " is at its most burning point. For this same Europe has made Christianity—the most delicate intensification and spiritualisation of Judaism—a deep and inseparable part of itself, and has adopted at the same time the humanitarian ideals of the classical philosophers, who had already opposed the naturalism inherent in current politics and in popular religion. Out of this curious combination of northern barbarism and Græco-Christian tender spirituality arose that remarkable phenomenon, Mediæval Europe.

Mediæval Europe resembles the mediæval periods of other civilisations in its agricultural and aristocratic character, in the smallness of its population and in the lack of the means of intercommunication, in the weakness of its administration and in its warlike spirit. But it combined all these things with the centralising and spiritually unifying force of the Catholic religion. The effect of this in theory, and to a large extent also in practice, was a form of politics religiously inspired and religiously controlled, the religion retaining all the time its supernational and humanitarian quality. A Christian community of peoples under the direction of a spiritual authority, the acknowledgment of the rights of all to life and health, an internal order and organisation according to classes, within each people, involving the care and consideration of the different classes of the community for each other, regard for the sacredness of human life and the infinite value of the soul, recognition of the freedom of the individual person and of its right to protection by the tribunal of the Church, and belief in the soul's complete and final independence of the world through love —an ideal presented in concrete form in the cloister and in the various international monastic orders—such were, in theory, and to a certain extent in practice, the characteristic features of the Middle Ages. If it did not succeed in putting this ideal into practice, the failure was attributed entirely to the sinfulness of human nature. That merely necessitated a renewed struggle against sin; it was never regarded as an indication that the theory was wrong. No wonder that such opposite schools of thought as the German Romanticists and the French Positivists should have regarded the Middle Ages as, in a certain sense, a permanent model for the constitution of Europe, or even for a world-order.

Nevertheless, this European Middle Age, surrounded as it was on all sides by richer and more powerful civilisations, such as the Byzantine and the Mohammedan empires, was but the first form and the beginning of European civilisation. In proportion as the various European nations became consolidated and formed national states and attained to a greater economic development, the unity of Christendom was broken up. The loosely organised communities consolidated themselves into firmly established sovereign kingdoms, and emancipated themselves in thought and feeling from the dominance of the Christian realm of ideas. Thus arose the absolute monarchy, with its centralised organisation, and thus, after Charles VIII's invasion of Italy, began the struggle to preserve the balance of power among the nations of Europe—in short, the whole modern political system of rival sovereign states which had freed themselves from the dominion of the Church, and had in a greater or less degree nationalised the various religious bodies, not only the Protestant ones, but even to some extent the Catholic Church itself. And it was this world of sovereign, monistically constituted, mutually antagonistic states, which, as a new thing in human history, marched victoriously forth to the ends of the earth, and began the subjugation and colonisation of the globe under European dominion. Hence that close complex of politics and economics, of imperialism, problems of population and imaginative outlook, which we have come to take for granted to-day.

This situation promptly received theoretical recognition and formulation. The essence of the doctrine of Machiavelli is not a piece of mere wanton immorality. It is a declaration of the emancipation of politics from the religious ethic and the religious universalism. Its moral features are due to the atmosphere of the Italian Renaissance. They are irrelevant to the main issue. But his doctrine of the autonomy of politics (the *ragione di stato*) is the decisive point. Political authority or statecraft, in the sense of the centralised, absolutist policy of the modern state, is a creation of force, both in internal administration and in foreign relations, and of necessity achieves its end by the means of continual wars. The logic of this doctrine of war and force was what had to be developed entirely from its own inner principle, with a simultaneous consideration of the geographical position of a state, the density of its population, and its economic conditions. The ethical significance of this for Machiavelli was the deliberate repudiation of Christian morality and its political ideals, and a return to the cultivation of the pagan virtues—Roman fortitude (*virtù*), the heroic heightening of the sense of life, and the evolution of an aristocracy of valour. It was irrelevant whether Machiavelli considered a republic or a monarchy the best form of government, for his republic would have been governed by a council of nobles, like Rome or Venice. His whole theory is ultimately based upon a profound contempt for the average man, who is regarded simply as material to be moulded by the powers of statecraft, and who may and should, if necessary, be mastered and controlled by moral and religious fictions.

A similar spirit is revealed in the celebrated reports of the Venetian ambassadors, the precursors and contemporaries of Machiavelli, which gave Leopold von Ranke his predilection for this age and its political outlook, completely opposed though it was to his own fundamentally Christian and humanitarian convictions. The same spirit is revealed again in all the great and able works on practical politics, propagating the theory of political expediency, which appeared in France and Italy side by side with the official Aristotelian political philosophy of natural right. Bocallini and Botero in Italy, Richelieu and the Duc de Rohan in France, stand out as apostles of this creed. Bacon and Hobbes represent the same trend of thought in England—the former

POLITICS, PATRIOTISM, RELIGION 145

cautious and hesitating, never quite divulging the secret of power, the latter betraying it in his ice-cold paradoxical way, and representing it as the logical outcome of the naturalistic philosophy.

True, this tendency in political life and literature was not allowed to develop without opposition. Devotion to the humanitarian ideals of the later classical age and Christian feeling rose in protest against it, a protest which found expression in the so-called Utopian literature, from the *Utopia* of Thomas More to the *Civitas Solis* of Campanella, or even to the treatises on eternal peace of the Abbé de St. Pierre and of Kant—works of which the socialistic Utopias of writers like Cabet and Fourier, or Bellamy's *Looking Backward*, are the sequel.

Yet precisely these Utopias illustrate very instructively the actual difficulties of the situation, and in this connection the first of them is particularly interesting—I mean that of your countryman, Thomas More. The first draft of his *Utopia*, written in Holland, is a clear and forcible expression of humanitarian feeling, inspired perhaps by his experiences during his political negotiations in that country. His traveller-hero, Raphael, tells of the wonderland he has discovered, where money is unknown and force is never exercised, and where the teachings of Christianity and classical antiquity are readily accepted, because they are closely related to the tradition of the country. It was evident that More would have liked to see his native England reformed upon this model; the resemblances between the island of Utopia and Great Britain have often been pointed out. Only an island is sufficiently isolated to permit of an ethical experiment of this kind. That may indeed be a hope for England, but it is a drawback to the general theory, and More himself had only the courage to apply his method to a distant land, and describes his hero as a dreamer—an illustration of the caution he considered necessary. Furthermore, the internal organisation of his ideal state is based on a system of slavery which relieves the citizens of all menial tasks, criminals, prisoners of war, or refugees being employed for the performance of these.

Moreover, More did not publish this first draft of his work. On his return to England he brought out in advance a new introductory section, expressing his repugnance for the Machiavellian policy pursued by a neighbouring Power, but suggesting, as in accordance with his own views, a practical middle course calculated to do justice to the actual requirements of the situation. He also appears to have introduced into the already finished main body of his work a number of modifications which are traceable from the manner in which they disagree with the context. Great stress, for example, is now laid upon the problem of over-population. Artificial methods of equalisation between one district and another are suggested as an immediate solution, but afterwards and above all conquest and colonisation. A theory of natural right is propounded, whereby thinly populated or little exploited districts may, in such circumstances, be occupied and defended by military force. In this way, however, he becomes involved in an intricate policy of war and alliance which, if carried to its logical issue, would not be very unlike that of Machiavelli himself.

He also champions the doctrine of an Apostolate of "Culture," according to which nations at a higher stage of civilisation have the right to bring reform, prosperity, and freedom to those at a lower level, whether these desire it or no. By this means the lower races are, however, brought under the rule and guidance of their liberators, a method which has repeatedly lent a sincere or a hypocritical justification to a policy of war and conquest, and in which the desire for power and prestige and the belief in the superiority and special vocation of a particular nation have found expression. This belief seems to be cherished in one form or another by every great nation and to coincide with its desire for expansion.

Finally, he turns his attention to the difficult problem known since Aristotle as the problem of the economic self-sufficiency of the nations. With this in view, he represents his Utopians as an agricultural community of the simplest possible type, exhibiting a freedom from desire for luxury or refinement which could never have been achieved in reality and which had already brought failure to Plato's ideal republic, the ideal scheme which served as a pattern to so many others. In the event of famine or the failure of crops, however, or if the food-supply provided by the country itself should prove insufficient, More advises a free interchange of goods, or, if this is not sufficient to meet the case, the exploitation of colonies and the creation of a reserve fund. Here again his counsels bear considerable resemblance to Machiavellian expedients.

In the main, then, More's *Utopia* represents a sincere endeavour to preserve the moral and religious standpoint, the methods he employs being the old Platonic devices with some additions derived from Christianity. But at the same time, it leaves notable openings for political realism (*Realpolitik*) or the doctrines of the *raison d'état*, by means of which all the theoretical problems and practical applications of Machiavellianism are able to penetrate into his system. Most instructive of all, however, is his reason for introducing these modifications and concessions. When he published his book he was himself entering upon a political career, and was about to become a member of the Privy Council. Not only did he find it expedient, therefore, to deal gently with the politicians, but he had also to consider what his own future policy was to be. In religion, indeed, he remained an idealist to the end ; and, in spite of the rather malicious criticisms which he had brought against the Church from the humanist point of view, he chose to die a martyr's death rather than support the subordination of the Church to the secular authority as a means of increasing the power of the State. It was as if fate had wished to lose no time in proving that political idealism is always punishable by death.

Similar comments would apply to all the Utopian literature of this period. What is most noteworthy, however, is that, in spite of the earnest thought which these writers gave to the subject, actual politics paid no attention to them. These actual politics took their course from the Franco-Austrian War of the Reformation period to the Thirty Years War, the English Civil War, and the War of the Spanish Succession, and subsequently from the European War in the reign of Frederick the Great to the Napoleonic wars, and from these to our last great World-war. Throughout all these vicissitudes they followed in the main the principles of Machiavelli, which seem to form an integral part of the doctrine of the balance of power. During the recent World-war the greatest minds of the age have wrestled with this problem and have suffered over it in ardent evocation of all its history and implications. To all appearance, however, even this world-upheaval has not proved a turning-point in history, but simply *one episode among others.* This sinister phrase indicates, I fear, the destiny that awaits us at the present time.

How is deliverance possible? Sincere and thoughtful men of all nations have asked themselves this question again and again in the last few years. Several alternative methods of solution lie before us. Unfortunately, however, they are very numerous and very different, and the limitations of each soon becomes apparent.

(1) In the first place, we might renounce idealism, and especially all idea of a universal religion, and content ourselves with a thoroughgoing naturalism. Machiavelli's periodic wars, such as those of the last few centuries of European history, would thus form a necessary element in the life of the great Powers. These Powers would not cease to fight for consolidation and extension of territory so long as they remained strong and prosperous. As they increased in strength they would carry their warfare to the remote parts of the earth and would be able for a while to locate it in such far and foreign regions, but would return home in the end, here to fight their most decisive battles against their neighbours. According to this outlook, the strongest and most prosperous nation, the nation most favoured by circumstances, would always conquer and would utilise its victory to the very uttermost, short of risking its own dissolution, and it would thus ultimately find a new opponent to dispute its claims. This procedure would continue as long as the system of competitive and conflicting forces retained sufficient power, and was able to keep going upon the natural resources of the globe. Should this power become exhausted, or should these resources fail, the whole fabric of civilisation would

crumble to pieces, having run its appointed course. God and the supernatural world are, according to this view, dreams, representing a fantastic, unrealisable ideal. " My kingdom is not of this world," said Jesus, and He knew what this implied, and acted in accordance with the knowledge. This political view is not, indeed, bereft of every ethical instinct, but its ethic is a heroic pessimism, recognising no end but glory and power and the fulfilment of destiny. This, indeed, is the ethic which already underlies Machiavelli's doctrine, and a similar view has lately been propounded in Germany by Otto Spengler in his book *The Decline of Western Civilisation*. " From Machiavelli to Spengler," that might well be the motto written by this mode of thought over the greatest and most tragic chapter of human history.

(2) The opposite solution is the purely religious and exclusively spiritual solution. According to this view, the Kingdom of God on earth possesses only the functions of suffering and of hope. The " Civitas Dei," or heavenly Jerusalem, consists in this world only of a small community of godly men and women who are represented by the Church. But just because the Church has to realise this mission under earthly conditions and in persistent

intercourse with earthly-minded men, it falls itself too easily into conflicts and schisms, into struggles for power and into the use of material means—in a word, into a worldliness of its own. But those to whom God has revealed Himself, those who have found salvation, will live in peace and charity with their neighbours, and suffer the rule of sin in the world until, at the end of this dispensation, the Kingdom of God shall appear, or until those who have remained faithful through suffering and sacrifice shall be reunited in heaven. This is Augustine's idea of the "Civitas Dei"; he has in view the heavenly Jerusalem, not the dominion of the Church upon earth. It is the view, again, of Sebastian Frank, the German mystic and opponent of Luther; also of George Fox and of many a later believer until the present day. It is characterised by the same heroism and pessimism as the doctrine of the extreme Machiavellians, but is directed to the realisation of the opposite values—hence its practical application yields an opposite result. You will find the same tradition running right through history, from the death of Jesus to the martyrdom of our pacifists to-day.

It is seldom that either of these solutions has been applied in practice without modification, and where this has been attempted it has always failed. Pure, unrestricted Machiavellianism leads the nations to their own mutual destruction and to universal mistrust. And against this tendency there stands men's need of mutual consideration and the moral sense of mankind. On the other hand, the purely spiritual ideal involves the renunciation of all attempt to gain control of the material world, and really indicates a lack of faith. Hence it too is seldom put into practice without compromises, as witness the several doctrines maintained towards the State and society by the various Christian Churches. All are, at bottom, compromises. Even the experiment of the saintly Quakers of Pennsylvania was a compromise, though too slight a compromise for it to be capable of enduring. In both cases men advocate theories which they do not put thoroughly into practice, or even follow out consistently in theory, and are ready to defend passionately doctrines in which only few wholeheartedly believe. The desire for theoretical simplicity is deep-rooted in human nature, and where men stand before a choice between alternatives, the simpler proposition is always preferred. Men can endure multiplicity in practical life, but not in their theoretical systems, though only madmen or fanatics, or the heroic champions of an entirely one-sided ideal, would seriously attempt to put such monistic theories into execution. Thus neither of these radically opposed solutions really comes within the range of practical possibility, the second even less than the first. Men have thus been obliged to devise other methods and have believed that they have succeeded.

(3) The third proposal is that of a united world-government or a single world-empire, guaranteeing peace to the nations. This empire would be ruled by a central governing body, allowing a certain autonomy to the individual States, but retaining authority to settle all disputes and guaranteeing the conditions of existence to every nation under its sway. The model of this solution is the Roman Empire, the first two centuries of whose rule have been celebrated by Gibbon in a famous chapter as the happiest period of human history, and it cannot be denied that it was during this period that Christianity and the Roman Stoic doctrine of natural right arose as correlatives of the ideal of a world-empire. Such an empire, however, entailed the destruction of the pride and independence of its constituent peoples, and was itself finally destroyed by its own weapons of military

defence, without which it could not have arisen, but with which it was impossible that it should endure for long. Further, belonging as it did to an age in which many of the races of mankind had not as yet come into communication with one another, there was no need for it to include more than a small portion of the world, it was based upon comparatively simple economic relations, and possessed a declining birth-rate.

At the present day an empire of this nature would have to include the greater part of the globe, and would have to control economic conditions and fluctuations of population over an immense area. And what Power could be equal to such a task? The Roman Empire collapsed through the inadequacy of its administrative technique, which was not sufficiently developed to meet the needs of its gigantic territory. How could a much larger area be administered to-day? And how would the older European nations, accustomed as they are to sovereignty and autonomy, endure such an administration so long as they preserved their present self-contained character? There is a book called *The Future of Mankind* by an American writer named Babson, in which this rôle is assigned to America, the greatest possible measure of democratic autonomy being guaranteed to the other half-co-ordinated, half-subordinated States. The writer recognises clearly enough, however, that the fluctuations in population, and the new economic requirements arising therefrom, would demand constant readjustments, which no constitution, however democratic, could avoid. Hence this method, too, seems unlikely to afford a solution, and is fraught with difficulties, even apart from the enormous sacrifice it would demand of the majority of the nations.

(4) If we reject the method of a central government, upheld by military force, there still remains the alternative solution of a voluntary mutual understanding, in other words, a League of Nations, supported only by treaties and the mutual goodwill of its members. This is a conception which is becoming increasingly popular as a result of the enormous technicalisation of modern warfare, and the tendency to substitute chemical and mechanical devices for military heroism. It may, indeed, prove a real solution, but it is exposed to one danger, viz. that where the constituent nations differ so much in strength, the League may simply prove an additional diplomatic contrivance in the struggle for supremacy. For remember, the Roman Empire itself was a league of nations. And even if this danger is

avoided, there remain the psychological difficulties resulting from the demand that the individual nations should renounce the sovereign power which has played so large a part in their political outlook since the sixteenth century. And there are, lastly, the insurmountable difficulties connected with the original distribution of territory and the present tendency to a redistribution of population. The nations are no longer isolated and self-contained nationalities, and that much more recent product, the consciousness of nationality, is in perpetual revolt against the natural geographical frontiers. The principles of national autonomy and the protection of minorities have so far seldom proved to be practical politics. They come into conflict with what the various States have in recent centuries believed and felt to be political necessity.

Above all, in view of the fluctuations in population and the constant migration, together with the corresponding changes in economic conditions, it is impossible to assume that the relative strength of the nations will remain unaltered, and this again entails changing economic circumstances. This last problem, which, as we have seen, proved the ruin of More's Utopia, would demand a perpetual redistribution of territory for which the necessary sympathy and goodwill would certainly be wanting. Even universal Free Trade would hardly relieve the situation, to say nothing of the fact that this too comes into conflict with modern theories of the State and Sovereignty, as soon as we have to do with some country whose command of trade and industry is not, apart from it, secure. It is not without significance that we should lately have been confronted with a new edition of that very Mercantile System which constituted the political economy of the absolute monarchy in the eighteenth century.

All these difficulties indicate the true path, that of practical compromise. Politics, which mean, and always must mean, the organisation of force both in the internal and the foreign activities of the State, which will to the end have to reckon with distrust in the dealings of one nation with another, which are always bound to look beyond the needs of the present generation, will never become free from certain basic characteristics, as these were actually perceived by Machiavelli. Politics spring from the natural constitution and the natural requirements of man. They are a piece of naturalism strained through the human intellect. But man does not live only upon the natural level, even in his political activities. Politics themselves must be capable of being brought, to a certain extent, into harmony with ethical and humanitarian conceptions ; in the home department there must be a recognition of the value of personality, and in dealings with other nations an acknowledgment of the claims of all to the necessaries of life. Otherwise politics can do nothing but further the barbarisation and mutual destruction of the nations. How this can be accomplished will depend in each case upon the special circumstances, and must thus be left to the genius of statesmen of imagination and insight.

I cannot deal with the question in more detail. It is enough that no general rules can be laid down. The important thing to recognise is that, above the sphere of politics and the natural man's gamble for power, there rises a realm of the spirit, of religion, which unites individuals belonging to different nations by forces and motives of an entirely different order. In this way there arises a unity and interconnection among men that operates in continual opposition to the demands of mere political expediency, which, for all its veneer of intellectual refinement, remains at bottom so crude. This realm of the spirit is of more delicate fibre than the realm of nature, hence it is easier to do it injury. At times it may even appear to be torn in pieces by the passions of men, but it is always restored in the end, for its foundations are broader and deeper than those of any political system, since thay are connected with a belief in the meaning and purpose of life which no politics can supply. Indeed, politics have a meaning only as conditioning and bringing into being a material environment in which the life of the spirit can flourish. Nevertheless, for this very reason the latter realm cannot fail in its turn to react upon the former, and, after all the catastrophes brought about by naturalism, it sets to work again to make the realm of nature serve its ends.

How this is to be done cannot, however, be stated in general terms. It depends upon the circumstances of the particular situation. Above all, it demands a courage, a loyalty and devotion, on the part of the representatives of religion, which shall carry them beyond all barriers of nationality. This method of compromise is aided, however, by an important discrimination, the nature of which I will now indicate as a conclusion to our whole discussion. The discrimination I mean is the discrimination between politics and patriotism. These are two essentially different things. Patriotism is the devotion to hearth and home, to one's own language and kindred. It is peaceful and individual—a quiet love of one's own type and customs. It is only with the increase of intercommunication and the growth of intellectual activity that this patriotism gradually develops into the block (monistic) conception of a nationality, embracing all who are related by blood or language, and uniting them in a common pride and loyalty. It has always been one of the principal devices of politicians, especially since the rise of modern democracy, to turn such feelings and passions to their own use. They have always contrived to make these far quieter, uncalculating emotions serve the purposes of their centralisings and ambitions, and have thereby succeeded in giving an ethical colour to their own exigencies or desires in the eyes and feelings of men at large. This, indeed, has often been quite justifiable.

Nevertheless, the two positions really remain distinct—a fact which becomes most evident in connection with the doctrine of national sovereignty. Modern politics draw their vitality from this conception, and adhere passionately to it. But naïve patriotism has no intrinsic need of it. All that it requires is opportunity for emigration, and respect for national liberty and honour. But, taken by itself, it could easily adapt itself to an international organisation and submit to limitations of the national supremacy, so long as similar conditions were accepted also by the other countries and did not signify the hegemony of any one single State. Such a severance of patriotism from politics (using the latter term in its modern technical sense) is in itself quite within the range of possibility, though it would involve a profound transformation in the structure and in the self-esteem of modern States which in the past were called into being by absolutism and which still to-day, in spite of all their democratisation, continue, in this matter, the absolutist tradition.

I read not long ago an English book called *The Foundations of Sovereignty*, by Harold J. Laski, in which this new conception is propounded, and it contains a list of other works where the same standpoint is adopted. Even in Germany, where the ill-defined and difficult geographical position of the country makes men readily find obstacles to their country's legitimate rights in any such conception, these questions are being widely discussed. In France the principle is defended by Duguit and Sorel. It may be that our whole political outlook is, at this point, undergoing a great inner revolution. This, however, will not bring the Kingdom of God upon earth, nor establish any Utopia, and there will still be room for the compromise I have suggested, though under such conditions it would perhaps be easier of execution. And, indeed, the administration of the traditions of absolutist politics by parliamentary democracies seems to have passed its zenith and to be less and less able to guarantee peace and order at home or abroad.

All these are practical problems which the scholar and thinker is not able to resolve. I can only try to indicate their theoretical aspect and to show its bearing upon the essentially theoretical problem we are discussing. This can find its solution only in a compromise between naturalism and idealism, between the practical necessities of human life upon earth and the purposes and ideals of the life of the spirit.

Many of us in Germany regard "compromise" as the lowest and most despicable means to which a thinker can have resort. We are asked to recognise a radical disjunction here, and to choose either *for* or *against*. And the further you go east the more noticeable this tendency becomes. But twist and turn the matter as you will, the fact remains that all intransigence breaks down in practice, and can only end in disaster. The history of Christianity itself is most instructive in this connection. It is, in the long run, a tremendous, continuous compromise between the Utopian demands of the Kingdom of God and the permanent conditions of our actual human life. It was indeed a sound instinct which led its founders to look for a speedy dissolution of the present world-order.

But there is a further point. In the last resort life itself, both purely animal existence and our human life, a dualism of body and spirit, consists in a constant, persistently precarious compromise between its respective constituent elements. And it is from out of this dual human life and out of its compromise that the highest heights of religious personality and of religious interdependence arise and grow. And in this their growth and struggle they point to a Beyond where they will at last be wholly free from earthly obstacles. This is the lot of humanity: human life is a struggle not only for physical existence or for the recognition of men's social and political rights. It is primarily a struggle between the life of nature and the life of the spirit that rises above nature and yet remains bound to nature, even whilst it turns against it. And if the whole course of history is thus characterised by compromise, it is not likely that the thinker can escape it. He, too, must confess to a compromise even in these days when this presence and need of compromise in all earthly things is weighing particularly heavily upon all our souls.

Amongst yourselves, in England, the principle of compromise is less undervalued. Political experience and the influence of empirical systems of thought have given you a different outlook, though you have not lacked your uncompromising thinkers, from the Puritan fathers to the disciples of Rousseau, Tom Paine, and Bentham. In spite of a natural distaste for a purely empirical philosophy, I have found this a particularly attractive and instructive feature of your literature.

It is thus easier for me to confess my adhesion to the principle of compromise here than in my own country. I know of no other principle and I am unaware of any practical thinker who does. It is true, however, that in the use of compromise we have to guard against all precipitate capitulation to the course which presents itself as momentarily expedient, or as the easiest way out of a difficulty, but which may be thus expedient and easy only for the moment, and, once more, we have to guard against any fundamental abandonment of the ideal. Indeed, it is only by keeping this ideal ever before our eyes that we can continue to hope and to strive for a better future in the midst of a cold and sinister world.

I should not like to bring these matter-of-fact reflections to a close without giving utterance to this belief and this hope. Only through faith, hope, and love can the *bellum omnium contra omnes*, to which nature and egoism incline us, be overcome. That is the inmost meaning of the Christian Gospel, although this same Gospel has always known well enough that the task, thus set to us poor little men, is far more difficult than any merely rationalistic optimism is ever willing to admit.

INDEX

The Arabic numbers refer to pages of the lectures; the Roman numerals refer to pages of the Introduction.

The entries are restricted to names of persons directly discussed or expressly appraised; to subject-matters emphasised or developed; and, for the Introduction, to explicit arguments and appraisements.

I
OF PERSONS

Aristotle:
    the teleological system and entelechy of, prove themselves by their fruits, 99

Augustine, St.:
    connects *lex naturæ* of Stoics with Neoplatonic theory of moral goods, 74
    brings the various goods, short of the *Summum Bonum* or *fruitio Dei*, under rubric of *uti, non frui*, 74, 75, 89
    his *Civitas Dei*, 152, 153

Comte (Auguste):
    fails to formulate world-process, 76, 93

Fox (George) and Franck (Sebastian): their purely spiritual outlook, 153

Hegel (G. W. F.):
    fails to formulate world-process, 93

Hobbes, Thomas:
    represents Machiavellianism as logical outcome of the natural philosophy, 144, 145

Jesus Christ:
   His declaration " He who is of the truth heareth My voice,"
      98
Kant (Immanuel):
   approximated ethical principles and logical principles too
      closely to each other, 47
   finally realised that unity of ethics deducible only from end,
      50, 51
   his phrase as to treatment of our neighbour as an end in
      himself, 54, 55
   pure intention of reasonableness required by, must be replaced
      by will to responsibility and decision, 65, 66
   wrongly holds antithesis between morality and nature always
      to involve pain, 84
   translates language of Concept of Nature into that of Concept
      of Moral Obligation, 103, 104

Machiavelli (Niccolò):
   his political doctrine emancipates politics from religious ethics
      and religious universalism, 142-144
   his whole theory ultimately based upon profound contempt
      for average man, 144
   opposition to, yet touches of, in More's *Utopia*, 145, 148, 149
   his doctrine of periodic wars, 151
More, Sir Thomas:
   analysis of his *Utopia*, 145-149
   significance of his death, 149

Plato:
   his idea of the Good proves itself by its fruits, 98, 99
   first to formulate damming of mere stream of historical facts
      by Ethic of Cultural Values, 104

Ranke (Leopold von):
   his inconsistency in admiring reports of Venetian ambassadors,
      144

Spengler (Otto):
   The Decline of Western Civilisation, 152

INDEX

Troeltsch (Ernst):
  his life, short sketch of, xi-xiii
    early sensitiveness to clash between history and metaphysics, 4-6
    became more and more super-denominational and, at same time, came more and more to regard specific kernel of religion as unique, independent source of life, 31
  his works:
    Fundamental Problems of Ethics (1902), xvi, xvii
    Protestant Christianity and Church (1906, 1909), xxi, xxii
    Separation of State and Church (1907), xix
    The Absolute Validity of Christianity (1909), 4-21
      his criticism of this work here, 21-28
      practical bearing of these modifications, 28-32
    The Social Doctrines of the Christian Churches and Groups (1912), 22, 23 ; xii
    The Historical Standpoint and its Problems, Vol. I (Sept. 1922), 23, 24 ; xiii
    The Place of Christianity among the World-Religions (Dec. 1922), 1-35 ; xviii-xxv
    Ethics and the Philosophy of History (Jan. 1923), 39-129, xxv-xxx
    Politics, Patriotism, and Religion (Dec. 1922), 133-167, xxx
  three preliminaries to study of these lectures:
    determination to treat his doctrines in spirit of his own oral teaching, xiii-xv
    recognition of changes from earlier outlook, xv-xvii ; xviii, 9-21, 28 ; xxi, xxii
    admission of some unintentional unfairness in treatment of recent English thought, xvii, xviii
  reminiscences of, as university teacher, by Albert Dietrich, xiv, xv
    as speaker amidst close friends, by Friedrich Meinecke, xxii, xxiii
  comparison of, with Plato, xxvii
    with Hegel, xxv, xxvi
    with Josiah Royce, xxix, xxx
    with Professor Eucken, xxvii

II
OF SUBJECT-MATTERS

Words with an asterisk preceding them are specially characteristic of Dr. Troeltsch's vocabulary and are mostly used by him in a precise and peculiar sense.

The terms " Eleatic fixity" and " salto mortale" occur frequently in the " Historismus" (September 1922), and the conceptions thus designated largely pervade the present lectures.

Absolute Validity of Christianity, The (E. Troeltsch), 4–31
Amoralism, historical relativism, does not lead to a fundamental, 66
Anarchy, rapidly increasing in religion and metaphysics, 120
Antitheses, the:
    between moral superstructure and natural basis different in morality of conscience, and in ethic of cultural values, 83, 84; 86, 87
Authority: 76, 77, 89
    survives in many forms through imitation and poverty of thought, 120, xxvi–xxx

Baptism, infant, Dr. Troeltsch's explanation of, xxvi, xxvii
*Beyond, the, a solution of all our problems, 129, 165
Buddhism and Confucianism rather philosophies than religions, 19
    without influence in political sphere, 137

Catholicism, mediæval, its endless conflicts, 116
China, religion of, genuinely moral under Confucianism, 138, 139
Christianity:
    in some degree a manifestation of the Divine Life, 26–28
    its capacity for and unpredictable course of development, 30, 31, xxi, xxii
Church, the:
    its attempt to comprehend all the social groups under single dome, 117–118
    Dr. Troeltsch's attitude towards, and sacraments, xvi–xx.
Churches, the:
    claims as to the other social complexes not realisable, 119, 123
    a common spirit of a metaphysical nature and, 123, 124

INDEX

*Combination, the personal, of morality of conscience and ethic of cultural values, 123, 127
Commandments, depend upon the commandment, 53-55
Common character of all religions unknown to history, 12, 13
Common spirit, the:
    its necessity, 107, 108; 117
    how it can develop from an individual procedure, 107, 108
    a religious, ethical, and artistic, actually existed in past as compared with present, 108, 109; 140, 141
    various conceptions of, 114, 117, 118
Communism and Socialism expect two miracles, 63, 64
*Complexes, social:
    the nine, in which we all live, 118-124
    united by the metaphysical-religious element alone, 123
*Compromise:
    unavoidable in all life upon earth, 64-66, 105, 164-167
    where, would be immoral, 66; 166, 167
    creative, 65, 111, 112
    how regarded in Germany and in England, 164-166
Confucianism and Buddhism rather philosophies than religions, 19
Conscience, a, ready to assume responsibility, 97
Consciousness, ethical, complexity of, its peculiarity, 47-49
    moral, the clearest element of ethics, 50
*Corporate personalities, 52, 53; 55, 56
*Creative act in synthesis of cultural values, 97
*Cultural atmospheres:
    a compromise adapted to successive stages of racial development, 111
    almost wholly individual systems, 83
Cultural sphere, one's own, 121, 122
*Cultural values:
    detachment from natural substratum of instincts, 84-87
    can be welded into homogeneous whole within large given areas of culture, 93-95

Danger from historical criticism to recognition of simple standards of value, as felt in Anglo-Saxon countries and in Germany, 7-9, 43
Darwinism, as enlarged into a Philosophy, 44
Decline of Western Civilisation, the, by Otto Spengler, 152

INDEX

*Differences, utter, found by Dr. Troeltsch between Western and Eastern Christianity, and between the world-religions, 22, 27; xx-xxi
*Discrimination between patriotism and politics, 161-167; xxx
Duties of solidarity, 103

Earthly history presupposition of final personal sanctification, but in itself a mixture of reason and natural instinct, 68
Eleatic fixity and *Heracleitan* evaporation, Dr. Troeltsch's attitude towards, xxvi-xxix
Emancipation from dominance of Christian ideas by the European nations, 142, 143
Empiricism and Nominalism, 3
    ethical, 44, 45
    monistic, its refutation, 45, 76
End, the, 50-53
Ernst Troeltsch, A. Dietrich, quoted, xiv, xv
Ernst Troeltsch and the Problem of the Historical Standpoint, F. Meinecke, quoted, xxii, xxiii
*Ethic of Cultural Values more difficult to construct as dams to flux of history than Morality of Conscience, 87, 95
Ethics:
    possible for, to be accomplished easily, 84
    struggle inseparably associated with, 105
    their irrevocable diversity, 105
    their qualities of compromise and individuality, 105
Ethical consciousness, extraordinary complexity of, 47-49
Eudæmonism, 54, 72
European civilisation:
    Christianity stands and falls with, 24, 25
    idea of Personality pre-eminently characteristic of, 99
Evolution and Progress, 41, 42

Force, the dogmatic:
    of universally prevalent ecclesiastical dogmas, 111
    shattered by churches replacing Church, 123
Free Trade, universal, and a League of Nations, 159
*Freedom:
    man's moral, would cease if morality ever simply victorious, 62
    determines everything in morality of conscience, 99
Fundamental Problems of Ethics, E. Troeltsch, xvi, xvii; xxv

INDEX

German humanistic and historical outlook, 4, 5
   and English tendencies to relativity—their different causes, 6-8
   poetry and the theory of ethical goods, 75, 77, 78
   Idealism, contrasted with thought of Western Europe, 75, 76; 90, 91; 104, 105; 112-114
      its constituents, 104
      fundamentally dissolved by Marx and Nietzsche, 113
     antipathy to compromise, 164, 165
Germ-cells of new spiritual freshness, need for, 125, 126
Good, the, effortless necessity of, something we cannot picture, 62
Goods or ends or values, 71, 72, 79
Gospel, the Christian, 167
Group, personality of, its reality and obligation, 55, 56
*Groups, only highly developed, transcend racial antagonisms, 61, 62

Hegelians, the English, Dr. Troeltsch's oblivion of, xvii, xviii
Historical Standpoint, the, and its Problems, E. Troeltsch, 23, 24; xiii, xvi
Humanity: doctrines of, 58, 103, 121
   concern men and groups as rational beings, 58

Imperfectibility of all ethical sciences, 106
*Individual, adj.:
   historical Christianity thoroughly, 22, 23
   relation of, historical facts to standards of value, similar throughout entire domain of history, 23, 24
   character of European civilisation and of Christian religion closely interconnected, 24, 25
*Individual, the, in foreground of religion, 67, 68
Individualism of Dr. Troeltsch, xix, xxiv, xxv, xxvii, xxix
*Individuality, its significance, 82, 83
Institutional element of religion, xvi, xxix, xxx
Intellectual class, predominance of, a result of culture, 112
International justice, 58
Islam, its racial character, 137

Judaism:
   and Zoroastrianism explicitly national religions, 18, 137
   interim, ethic in, 137

Jus naturæ, the Christian, of the lawyers, 90
Justice, international, 58
*Justification by faith, present in ethics and research, 67, 68, 98, 99, 111
Justitia civilis and *Justitia spiritualis*, 74

Kingdom of God, the:
    lies beyond all history, 68, 129
    Christianity and the, 165

Lay theories of culture require faith, 99
League of Nations, a, difficulties as regards, 157-159
Liberalism, its ordinary and its nobler kinds, 107, 108, 110

*Mankind, all, no goal common to, can be found, 93
Methodism and Pietism, the apologetic produced by, 10
*Middle Ages, the European, 109, 140-143
Miracles, 9, 10, 12, 15, 16
Missions, foreign, 28-30
Modern society, possible to dam flux of history on basis of, 110
Monarchy, the absolute, anti-Christian, 142
*Monistic:
    empiricism, its refutation, 45, 76
    conceptions of the common spirit, delusive, 117, 118; 126
    theories as to relations between politics and religion, 154, 155
Moral consciousness:
    the clearest element of ethics, 50
    two distinct questions as to, 59-64
Morality:
    universal, essentially a perpetual struggle, 62, 63; 84
    can never be simply victorious and thus end freedom, 62, 63
    always transcended by religion, 62, 63; 67, 68
    *of conscience and ethic of cultural values, main difference between, 82, 83; xxv, xxvi
    question as to use of terms "morality" and "ethic," 77
    difference in relation of moral superstructure to natural basis between, 83-85

*National community, the, what it really requires, 122, 158
Nationalism, modern, a monistic exaggeration, 122; 151, 152

INDEX 177

Natural instincts, their justification in human nature, 63
Neoplatonism and cultural values, 74, 89, 104
Nominalism, touches of, in Dr. Troeltsch's outlook, xx, xxi

Objectivity present in damming history by ethics, 106, 107; 167
Originality, more, and more community demanded by modern conditions, 124

Pacifists, our present day, 153
Pantheistic concept, the, in Schleiermacher and Hegel, 90, 91
Past, sentimental fancy in romantic idealisations of, 108, 109
*Patriotism and politics, 161–164
*Personalities, corporate, 52, 53; 55, 56
*Personality:
    the achievement of, 51, 52
    of the group, its reality and obligation, 55, 56
    a Western belief, but for us the truth, 99
    as Freedom determines everything in morality of conscience;
        as Object, everything in ethic of cultural values,
        51, 99
Place, the, of Christianity among the World-Religions, E. Troeltsch, 1–35; xviii
Pleasure, 72, 84
Politics:
    meaning of term, 134, 159
    where religion is national and where ethical, 134–138
    in Confucianism and mediæval Christianity, 137–141
    under emancipation from Christian ideas, 141–150
    the four possible attempts to solve problem, 150–159
    and ethics and patriotism, 160–164
    need of carefully limited compromise, 164–167
Progress and Evolution, 41, 42
Protestant Christianity and Church, E. Troeltsch, xxi, xxii

Realm of Spirit and realm of Nature, 160, 161
*Relativism, historical, how far transcendable by morality, 66–69
Religion always transcends morality, 62, 63; 67, 68
Renaissances of ecclesiastical or rationalistic dogmas, 108
Rights of Man, origins of doctrine of the, 58, 103

Salto Mortale, the, xxiii, xxiv ; xxvii, xxviii
Scepticism, 106, 107
Sciences, the " systematic mental," and ethics, 80-82
Selfishness of group not more venerable than of individual, 56, 57
Separation of State and Church, E. Troeltsch, xix
Social Doctrines of the Christian Churches and Groups, E. Troeltsch, 22, 23 ; xii, xv, xxii, xxvi
Socialism, 63, 64 ; 119, 120
Sociological structure, the, in successive cultural epochs, 114-116
*Sovereign state, idea of the, expressive of emancipation from Christian outlook, 142, 143 ; 162, 163
*Spheres, two different, of moral consciousness, 77 ; 78-80 ; 165
*Standards of value, difficulty of establishing, not confined to religion, 23, 40
Stoics, their error concerning pain, 62, 84
*Stream, the endless, of historical life, requires limitation by fixed standards, 39, 51, 129
*Struggle, universal morality a perpetual, 64, 65 ; 105, 165
*Synthesis, a conscious, of cultural values, how attained, 95-98 ; 124

*Tension, ethical life and Christian sphere of culture, full of interior, 46, 92, 95
Tolerance, present-day, languid, philosophic, 107, 110
Tribal and national religions, 134-136
*Truth :
    for us does not cease to be very truth and life, 26, 34, 99
    in God is one, in human experience is many, 34, 35
    polymorphous, not *monomorphous*, xix-xxi

Unity of modern mind more diversified than mediæval, 126
Universal :
    whether Christianity exists, in all the religions, irrelevant if not ultimate truth, 15, 16
    recognition of, as present in all religions, not strictly provable, 16, 17
Universality :
    tendency of history not towards, 14, 34
Utopia, More's, 145-149
Utopian literature, actual politics paid no attention to, 149, 150

INDEX

*Validity :
    ultimate, Christianity's claim to, 25
    distinction between, in itself, and validity *for us*, 26, xix–xxv
    other religions may possess their own, 26, 28
    the final objective of, lies beyond all the religions, 31, 32

Value :
    relative, of the several religions, impossible to determine, 27, 28, xix–xxv
    central cultural, in China, India, Greece, Rome, and Christianity, 94, 95

Values :
    an abiding system of, 42, 43
    ethical cultural, are entirely historical creations, 80
    a system of, how evolved, 94, 96, 97

Western Europe :
    thought of, contrasted with German Idealism, 75, 76 ; 90, 91 ; 112–114, xvii, xviii
    its general character, 104, 105

World :
    empire, difficulties of a, for our day, 155–157
    process, we simply cannot formulate the, 92, 93
    religions, distinguished from crude heathenism, 28–30
        relations really possible between, 33, 34
    War, the, to all appearance, only one episode among others, 150

Youth, leagues of, their special present-day function and task, 124, 125, 128

Zoroastrianism and Judaism, explicitly national religions, 18, 138